$ELLING
$ECRETS
THAT
$HOW YOU THE
MONEY!

$ELLING $ECRETS THAT $HOW YOU THE MONEY!

◆

This book is written for the benefit of All "Outside Salesmen" and Sales Managers

Robert H. Felgen

iUniverse, Inc.
New York Lincoln Shanghai

$ELLING $ECRETS THAT $HOW YOU THE MONEY!
This book is written for the benefit of All "Outside Salesmen" and Sales Managers

iUniverse books may be ordered through booksellers or by contacting:

iUniverse
2021 Pine Lake Road, Suite 100
Lincoln, NE 68512
www.iuniverse.com
1-800-Authors (1-800-288-4677)

The views expressed in this work are solely those of the author and do not necessarily reflect the views of the publisher, and the publisher hereby disclaims any responsibility for them.

The author and publisher specifically disclaim any liability that is incurred from the use or application of the contents of this book.

ISBN-13: 978-0-595-40872-6 (pbk)
ISBN-13: 978-0-595-85236-9 (ebk)
ISBN-10: 0-595-40872-9 (pbk)
ISBN-10: 0-595-85236-X (ebk)

Printed in the United States of America

Contents

Acknowledgments

My love and thanks to my wife, *Ann*, without whom this book would still be in my computer in rough draft and would not be in your hands now. Having the street smart knowledge and typing it into a computer is easy as I know the subject well. It was *Ann* who set it up in publisher's condition. Ann has a full-time job as Human Resources Director for an Aerospace Company and also must spend many hours every week studying for a series of eight courses and exams to qualify for the "CEBS" (Certified Employee Benefit Specialist) program which is equivalent to a "Masters Degree" in Human Resources.

Also, thanks to my Mother, *Lenore,* who was an extra special Mother to my brother, Tom and I. She worked at home typing business letters to put us through college. Mom found time to write a book titled *"How You Can Earn $10,000 Typing At Home?"* To my father, *Harold,* ("Mike") who worked for the telephone company in Chicago for 45 years and who was the nicest father in the world. Also, thanks to my brother *Tom*, a friend and pal with a wonderful sense of humor, and who has won two international barbershop quartet championships as a bass singer with *"The Four Renegades"* and *"Chicago News."* Tom and I went to grade school at St. Catherine of Siena in Oak Park, Illinois with comedian Bob Newhart. *Tom* also made suggestions that are incorporated in this book.

I also owe a big *thank you* to *Brandy* and *Jim Foust* of the *Sacramento Movie Company* for the technical help they gave me and for the *cover* and *web-site design* for my book.

Finally, to our seven wonderful children *Todd, Laurie, Shelly, Forrest, Brandy, Tony* and *Nick,* whom I love dearly and the thought of whom kept me going forward through thick and thicker. (There is no "thin" in selling!)

I would like to acknowledge my admiration for *Mr. Louis Brunner,* founder and President of *The Brulin Company*, who, although trained as a chemist, created the "culture" at *Brulin* which, to all the salesmen, was truly a *"salesman's company."* My thanks to *Bob Brunner*, Louis Brunner's son and Vice President at that time, who *made me an offer I couldn't refuse* to change jobs to become a sales manager for his specialty chemicals company.

I want to thank *John Kirk*, an unsung "inside" national sales manager, who knows everything to support his outside sales force throughout his many years' service. John retired in 2005.

I give a lot of credit for my success to the very fine and knowledgeable chemists who educated me, and others, including customers, in the products they created and we sold. My thanks go to *Julius Neuberger, Hiram Gooch, Dennis Zupan, John Roudebush, Joe Adams, Bob Grange, Don Olson, Dick Miller, Don Morco of the Brulin Company and Pat Scalera, chemist with the Henkel Corporation, Aerospace Division.*

I also want to acknowledge my *admiration and support* in the creation of this book *for salesman and sales managers of all ages everywhere.* The selling profession is a very good life for those who do it right, enjoy it, become *"Street Smart"* and prosper.

I would like to give recognition to the *"Master Salesmen"* I have worked with or have known of during my sales career. These salesmen, like the "Masters" in golf, are *"Masters of Selling"* and I honor them here for their life-long superior achievements in the selling profession.

"MASTER SALESMAN'S CLUB"

This is the *"Medal of Honor"* of *"SALESMANSHIP"* to those men and women who have endured the test of time in the selling profession and have mastered the techniques, within their own personalities, of persuading all kinds of people to give them money for an item or service they thought they didn't need or want before hearing their golden words.

So the *"Master Salesman"* has found a way to succeed in the selling profession and have succeeded in a very tough, competitive business through the ever-changing years. They have successfully made it all the way through the *"minefield of selling"*!

Hank Bonsall, Seattle, San Francisco, Carroll Buckley, Cleveland, Joe Carter, Dallas, Jack Casey, President, Indianapolis, Hoytt Childress, Miami, Jeff Cornes, Tampa, Doc Eddy, North Carolina, Bob Felgen, Aircraft Sales Manager, Western Regional Sales Manager, Vice President National Accounts, Joe Ferguson, Minnesota, Mike Frisce, San Antonio, Barry Gilberg, Detroit (Warner's), Don Henderson, Georgia, Frank Houser, Los Angeles, Andy Kearney, Seattle, Alaska, Joe Knue, Indianapolis, Vic Landis, Los Angeles, Russ Lindersmith, Orange County, CA, Gordon Malone, Arizona, Dan Mannion, Los Angeles, Pat Mannion, Southern CA Sales Manager, National Sales Manager, Don McClellan, Chicago, Bob McClure, Tennessee, Mac McDaniel, Atlanta, "T-Bone" McDonald, Oklahoma, Charlie Merrick, Dayton,

Jack Mills, Detroit, Donald Olson, Chicago, Detroit & Minneapolis (Warner's), Mike Polocheck, Gary, IN, Ron Puszynski, St. Louis, Leo Ray, Seattle, Jack Redlich, San Francisco, Bob Ritter, Baltimore, Don Robb, Western PA, Keith Sadler, Oregon, Arkansas, Ted Sass, Wisconsin, Ralph Sauder, Southern, IL, Jim Savell, Louisiana, Joe Scarpa, Eastern PA, Tom Seavey, Los Angeles, Boyd Smith, Assistant National sales Manager, Frank Torok, Western Aerospace Sales Manager (Henkel), Joe Vandenbark, Indianapolis, Ron Wakefield, Greater Los Angeles Area, East, John Ward, Midwest Regional Sales Manager, National Sales Manager, Jim White, Western Los Angeles County and Central California Coast, Don Williams, Utah, Nevada.

CONGRATULATIONS!

Author's note: I have asked several "Master Salesmen" to contribute their "War Stories" and "Secrets" of their selling success to this book. Their secrets to success are given away in chapter twenty five.

Preface

It is a salesman's gift to himself as a result of possessing all the components of selling, that a salesman can *see* opportunities for extra sales that are invisible to all others. This *extra perception,* that is unseen and untaught, is one talent that makes the vast difference in a professional salesman's selling performance over and above all the rest.

This book offers *you,* the reader, many examples and stories illustrating this extra perception in *"seeing"* unusual opportunities for the *extra sale.* There are many other examples of thinking outside the normal sales box to achieve huge sales increases over and way above the "expected" daily selling routine of above average selling.

This book gives you, the experienced salesman or sales manager, ideas and stories of actual examples of how these major sales were constructed. This book tells you how to beat all competitors and rise to *No.1* in your corporation in *sales increase, sales volume and commissions and bonuses earned.* This book gives away the *"secrets"* of how this can be achieved. It is up to you, if your desire is strong enough, to motivate yourself to do the *necessary work* that is required to sell yourself to *"No.1"* and enjoy the big money and other rewards you will have earned.

'Salesmen or Salespersons'

"Salesman" has for all-time meant anyone who sells goods or services—"Death of a Salesman" it's not Death of a Salesperson! *In this book, a "salesman" is any man or woman who is selling goods and services as their profession.*

1

The Pyramid of Selling

1. The 'Pyramid'

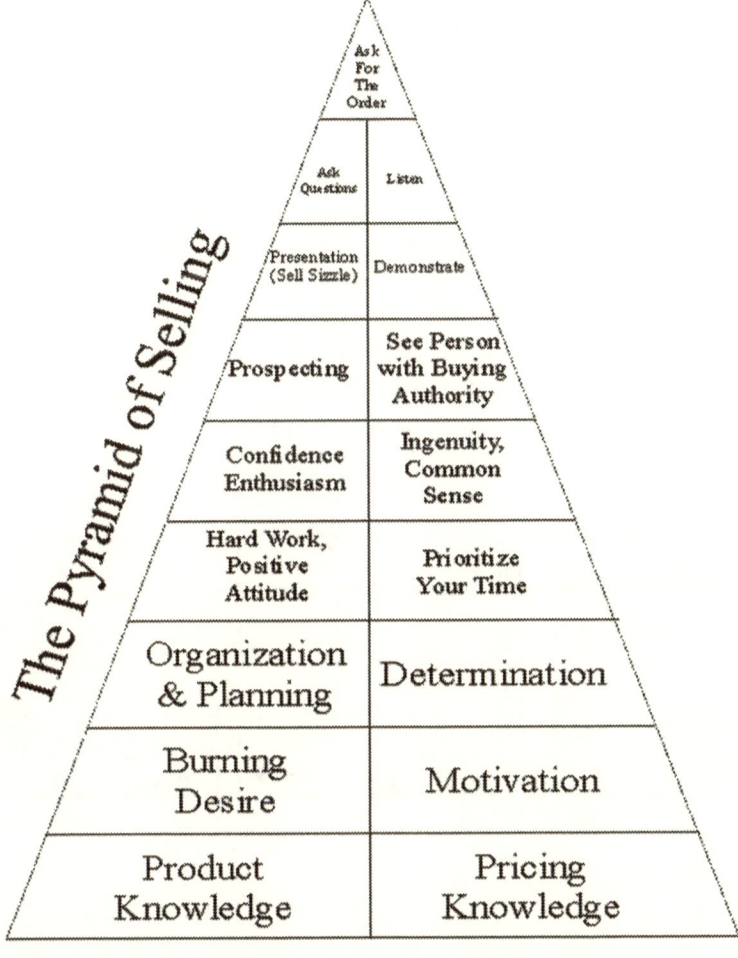

2. 'Dark Energy'

There are some universal basic truths in selling, as shown in 'The Pyramid of Selling' and many untold truths a salesman learns from successful experience. The reasons for most successes in selling are invisible like the "dark energy" in the universe. We can't see it, we don't talk about it, but it is real and can *make the difference* in getting the sale even after the basics of selling have been utilized.

3. The 'Force'

The Book, "Selling Secrets That Show You The Money!" will cover the basics in "The Pyramid of Selling" and talk about and site examples of the elusive *"dark energy"* that makes the difference in selling. A salesman can utilize all the known published steps in selling and will probably succeed, but like Luke Skywalker in "Star Wars" before the *"force"* was with him. The *"dark energy"* is the *"force,"* the *"secrets"* in selling, because *"salesmanship"* is elusive and personal.

We could program a robot with most of the basics of successful selling but we can't program that *"fourth dimension", "dark energy,"* which is *talent* or *"salesmanship".* On the other hand, the *"force"* can be with you but without the basics of selling, would be like going into battle without the "light saber." You have the *"force,"* but no weapon. You need both to succeed to the highest level and this book gives you both the "Pyramid of Selling" and stories where the elusive *"fourth dimension," the "dark energy" or "the force"* that makes the difference, is utilized. The basics of selling, a salesman's experience and *"the force"* all together, smooth and seamless, is called *"salesmanship."*

Dilbert: © Scott Adams/Dist. by United feature Syndicate, Inc.

2

Building Anything Begins With a Foundation

1. A Fine Kettle of Fish You've Gotten Me Into

"You have a nice smile." "You ought to go into sales!" Forty-seven years later, the sales profession has been good to me, but it's a hell of a way to choose a profession. After four years of college, I was like Sergeant Schultz from the television series "Hogan's Heroes"—*"I know nothing!"*

"You're a natural salesman" is often pinned on any decent-looking person with an out-going personality. It's helpful, but it doesn't mean a thing in selling your way to the No. 1 spot in sales and income in your company. I rate it as one tenth of 1 percent of what you need to know and do to be No. 1. I've seen a "Billy Goat Gruff" and the "Troll that lives under the bridge" types become the No. 1 salesman in several organizations. Simply, it takes *thorough knowledge of your products and people and the other 99.9 percent hard work, planning and a burning desire to do it.* I'll repeat it, as in my experience, it's the key to success: *"A burning, almost fanatical desire!"* You will let *nothing* stop you!

2. Product Knowledge

Product knowledge is the base of the "pyramid" in successful salesmanship. How can you convince someone to part with big money if you don't know anything about your product except that it is "fantastic?" Product knowledge instills great confidence in the salesman and in the prospect.

- Why is my product better than what the prospect is using?

- What is he or she using?

3

- What price is he paying? (You might not get answer to this one.)

- Does he pay freight?

- From what city or country does he pay freight?

- How long does his current product last?

- Is it safe?

- Is my product safer?

- Why?

- How is the prospect's vendor's service?

- Why should the prospect buy your product?

You must know why the prospect will be better off with your product and you must tell him for his own good—and yours.

You can be handsome, beautiful, well dressed, well educated and well spoken, but if you don't know why the prospect should buy your product, you are wasting your own and your prospect's time. It's like begging. "Buy my product, please, because it will help me." "Thanks for stopping, but no thanks!"

Demonstrate, use your product yourself and get hold of, buy and try your competitor's product if possible. You will find out your product is much better in many ways and you can now list the benefits with pure enthusiasm. Ask yourself what you would want if you were in the prospect's place. Tell him how buying your product will benefit him and his company. Tell him how your service will be of benefit to him. Paint a picture of the benefits in his mind. What will these benefits do for your prospect and his company?

Think of product knowledge as a sword with which you are going into battle. You not only have to understand what the sword is made of, the weight and its balance, of vital importance is practice in how to use it to its best advantage. You must learn everything about sword fighting technique and practice, practice and practice some more. You'll be up against experts whose product knowledge of the sword and how to use it are legend. It is the same with your products. Learn all you can about them, use them, demonstrate them, learn their features and their benefits, your pricing versus your competitor's and point by point exactly why your product is better. Do this and you will slay the dragon.

To be successful in sales there are many factors and probably the most important is product knowledge along with pricing knowledge, without which the sale probably won't be made. You must know your product inside and out. You must know all its features, and why these features are benefits to the buyer. Product knowledge goes beyond your own product.

For example, if you sell Mercedes-Benz, a prospect that is interested and comes into your showroom and is probably trying to be sold on whether to buy a Mercedes, Lexus, BMW, Lincoln or Cadillac, the salesperson must thoroughly know all the features of the Mercedes and of what benefit these features will be to the prospect. He must fully understand the pricing structure he has with which to work. The Mercedes-Benz salesman must also know the features and pricing of the cars being considered to be able to tell the prospect why he should choose the Mercedes. The salesman should not mention the other car's features that may be less desirable, if the buyer doesn't bring it up. That might put an idea into his head to look at the other "comparable" cars. He came in to buy a Mercedes-Benz, unless the salesman chases him away. The sales representative must *paint a picture* of the other non nuts and bolts benefits of owning a Mercedes-Benz. Then demo the Mercedes, pointing out the benefits of all the many unique features. Let him or her drive the Mercedes and feel the power, prestige and thrill, then *"close"* the sale while he is favorably and emotionally influenced.

The salesman will have done this prospect a big favor. He will love his new Mercedes-Benz and be proud to be seen driving it. He will be glad "he" made the decision to buy his new Mercedes-Benz.

If the prospect leaves without buying the Mercedes, the sales representative is letting other sales reps at the above car dealers tell "his prospect" why their cars and deals are better, or make him a deal he can't refuse. The Mercedes-Benz Sales Representative will probably never get a second chance! The salesman is selling one of the best, most prestigious cars in the world. Tell the prospect about all the benefits he or she will receive, demonstrate it and write the order.

3. 'Features and Benefits'

Of course, you should know all the features and benefits of the products you sell. Some salesmen think you have to memorize them and present all of them to every prospect. Know all of your features and benefits, but tailor them to each individual prospect's needs and interests, which will be more interesting to him. Always use common sense and tell the prospect how your product will benefit him and his bottom line. You should resist any pressure to have you come in like a robot to present a "canned" sales presentation. Put canned sales presentations back in the can. They have no place or effectiveness in professional sales. Know the benefits your product will give to each prospect; tell them about it and ask them to try it.

4. Factors that Help a Salesman Become Successful

The list that follows encompasses some of the factors that help a salesman become successful. Incorporate them into your sales practice and you'll soar to *No. 1 and the gold.*

1. *Desire,* in fact, a *burning desire,* to be the best salesman in the whole company! Being the best is not easy. When you have the desire, you will find a way to overcome all obstacles and keep going. With the desire to succeed, nothing will discourage you. You will keep pressing onward no matter what. You've got to want to!

2. A *competitive spirit* in selling as in sports compels a salesman to win at all costs. It motivates a salesman to go way above and beyond mastering the basics of selling and forces him or her to a higher level over persons that are not competitive. People are either very competitive or they are not competitive! The competitive person will win every time because he or she must win the battle at all costs!

3. *Confidence.* As the *"burning desire"* pushes you to accomplish more, you become more confident and nothing can stop you. When a salesman shows confidence in himself and his products, the prospect is reassured and is also more confident in going ahead with what you are asking him to do. On the other hand, a lack of confidence, which comes from not knowing the product well enough, will lose an otherwise potential sale. *Sell with confidence.* It's reassuring to the prospect.

4. *Product knowledge.* Without it, you can't sell it! Read your own literature first. Get a sample. Try it out yourself. Ask yourself why you would buy it. Is there any reason you would not buy it? Why? What is the competition selling to compete with my product? What do their products cost? Ask your Sales Manager why the price of our product is higher than most competitive products. There is a good reason. Find out. Demonstrate your product. You

will be amazed with how wonderful your product really is. Now you can present it with enthusiasm and confidence.

5. *Enthusiasm.* "Enthusiasm is catching!" A sales representative can acquire very good product knowledge, but if he gives the prospect all the facts about his product, but without any enthusiasm, it is hard for the prospect to get excited about or buy the product. It is human nature to admire true enthusiasm. It is the exact opposite reaction to the unenthusiastic. If you know your product inside and out and truly know and believe it is the best product in the world, how could anyone who calls himself a salesman not be enthusiastic? The dictionary defines enthusiasm as "lively, absorbing interest or involvement" and *"something inspiring enthusiasm."*

6. *Organization.* Keep a file for every customer and prospect. Create a file for a prospect when there is correspondence or a price quote. It is helpful to have a copy of your account sheet in front of each file so you have all important information always with the file. Buy a file cabinet. File by account name or by name and by city. Take the files that have quote information or other information you will need, on each call. If you are asked about information you have in your file you will have it at hand. Keep these files neat and in order by date so you can find information you are looking for in front of a customer or prospect. If you are organized, you will look organized in front of your customer or prospect. This instills confidence in you, your prospects and customers.

Keep your account book up to date, making notes after each sales call to help you on your next sales call. Post your orders from the invoice copies each weekend to the sales sheets. You will always have the latest ordering history on your account sheet with you on your next trip. Keeping the order history tells you if the orders have dropped off and you can ask why. Also, you can see the products each account has ordered and sell them your best selling items that they don't have. The up-to-date account sheet tells you all the pertinent information you need to write an order without having to ask every time. Name, address, zip code, shipping information, attention to whom, designated truck line, pallets and shrink wrap required, etc., will all be entered on the account sheet in the three-ring binder or the company's printed sheets and binder.

Keep a good loose-leaf calendar or soft cover calendar book with you to enter next appointments and promises to be kept. Franklin-Covey planner is the best I have found. It is expensive as planners go, but how much is it worth to your income to be perfectly *organized?* To locate a Franklin-Covey store near you, call 800-360-8118.

5. A Salesman's Income

There are many different pay plans for a salesman, but most boil down to two basic plans.

1.   Straight commission with a "draw" (called "draw against commission").

2.   Salary and company car plus expenses.

Both plans offer "carrots" or bonuses for sales that exceed quotas to add some motivation other than keeping your job. New salesmen prefer salary and company car, which offers more security and continuity of income for a young family just starting out. The starting salary is usually not high, but a company car and all expenses are worth money the salesman and his family will not have to spend.

"Draw against commission" means the salesman is paid a set amount of money every month, regardless of commission earned from that month's sales. But, it is not a free ride! If the salesman is paid more in draw in a month then the commissions he has earned, the salesman will be in the "*RED!*" He will owe that amount to the company. The next month, if his commissions are more than his draw, the *"red"* amount will be deducted and the salesman will receive the difference. If in the *"red"* the second month, the amount is added to the first month's *"red"* amount and the salesman is starting to dig himself a hole. Companies go along only so far if the salesman doesn't show good improvement and potential and gets himself too deeply into the *"red."* If a salesman is floundering and in and out of the *"red,"* the company sometimes keeps any commission overage in the salesman's account to hedge against any further deficits. If a salesman is deep in the *"red"* and, with little or no hope of ever receiving any commission overage money, he gets discouraged. This is reverse incentive, and this salesman will either be let go or will quit.

On the other hand, to a good or more experienced salesman, "straight commission" is the only way to go. It gives *you* the chance to earn as much as you want or are able to earn. You drive your own car, pay most, if not all, of your own expenses, and have more freedom to do it your own way to maximize your income, and your business expenses are tax deductible. There is no bigger incentive anywhere when, on every Monday of every week, you have *zero* on your weekly commission check! You have to plan and scramble to sell enough every week to build another great commission check. You may still choose to get a small draw check with which to run the house, but to you that isn't even money. You are at *"zero"* on Monday! There is no bigger incentive or "carrot" than *straight commission.* It's like jumping into the ocean without a life preserver! If you're good, try it! I did it and it worked very well for me through the years.

3

How Much Is It

1. Pricing Knowledge

Just as important as product knowledge is *pricing knowledge*. Know your pricing policy inside and out. Know before you go in just how far you are willing to discount if the situation, in your estimation, demands some give and take to land this prospect as a customer. You must know beforehand from your Sales Manager if you can give a bigger discount if required to land a big deal. You must know how this will affect your commission. If your normal commission is 20 percent on a "list price" or "book price" sale and you are authorized to discount up to 10 percent, and you do, what commission will you receive? You should receive 20 percent of the new lower selling price.

Some commission plans list a "salesman's cost" amount in code in the price book and a list or selling price for each item. The difference between the two prices is the salesman's commission in dollars and cents. For instance, if the selling price of an item is $10.00 and the salesman's cost is $8.00, his commission is $2.00 per item. If the item is discounted 10 percent and the new selling price is now $9.00, the commission drops to the difference between the new selling price and the salesman's cost. The new commission is $1.00 per item instead of $2.00. The "salesman's cost" amount is the companies cost which they must get to pay all their expenses of manufacturing, shipping, salaries, a profit and all other expenses. If the salesman cuts the selling price, he cuts his commission accordingly. In effect, this salesman has to eat a 50 percent cut in commission to offer a 10 percent discount to get the order for his company. Some companies will *split the discount with the rep,* so discounting 10 percent costs the rep only a 5 percent loss of his commission. On very big accounts that may require a discount bigger than 10 percent, the Sales Manager may offer the salesman a *flat rate* commission percent. If the company and the salesman give a 25 to 30 percent discount to get a large volume account, the salesman will only receive a 5 percent commission or less. The salesman must receive enough commission to cover his time it will take to service this major customer.

You must know your pricing policy inside and out! If you sell a prospect on your product and, when asked how much it costs and you have to stop the momentum and thumb through your price book, as in fishing, you have *"slacked the line"* and probably lost the sale. It doesn't instill buyer confidence, after being told the item in question is the company's best-seller, *if you don't even know the price.*

You must know the quantity discount schedule so you can *"sell-up"*. If the buyer can pay less if he buys in bigger quantities, *he ought to be offered the chance.* He will be pleased that you offered a way to save money *and you get a bigger order.* This also keeps competition from catching him with low stock and stealing a "trial order." Your customer is not going to try something new when he has a lot of inventory. Also, if you are up against price and you are quoting on one item and the prospect tells you he is getting a lower price, *you should ask how many does he have to buy to get that price and does he have to pay the freight?* If that's a ten-item price and you are quoting on one unit, you will lose the sale. *If you know your quantity pricing and freight policy, you can get the order and a new repeat customer.* He's used to buying ten items at a time, so don't quote on fewer than ten items. If your ten-item price is the same or more, then try for 15 or 20 items to beat the competitor's price. If this customer pays freight and your plant or warehouse is in the same city, *you can greatly cut his freight costs.*

You must know your price/discount schedule. If all mentioned above doesn't work and you are still even with competition, know what you can discount to get the order. How much of a discount would induce a change in vendors? How far can you go within company policy? How much can you discount and still earn a decent commission? *Don't give away the farm to get an order.* Figure how much a 5 percent discount on 20 items equals in dollars saved for the prospect. Reinforce your savings with the quality of your product and service, freight-savings dollars, 50 percent reduced invoice costs and the proximity of your factory will benefit him by fast or emergency deliveries and finally, your close availability for good, fast service. *Ask for the order!* (You have *earned it!*)

"I am happy with the product I'm using now and *your price is higher.*" At this point it really pays to know your competition's quality reputation. Instead of giving your higher quality product away to match the competitor's price, *detail the added value* that your product will give to him compared to the competitive product. In selling industrial chemical cleaners or anything, *knowing your business* can reverse the discounting situation. If your company's industrial cleaner is colored light blue or light red, and the competitive product is dark red or blue, the customer's *perception* is that the darker cleaners are stronger or more powerful. Dye is cheap and the dye doesn't do any cleaning. *"Actives" or "solids"* do all the cleaning work *and the rest is water.* Some industrial cleaners contain only 3 to 5 percent actives with a lot of dye to make them look strong and sell for more than they are worth. Also *there are quality "actives" and cheap actives.* The cheap actives are harsh on the items to be cleaned and the people who use them.

Quality cleaners contain 18 to 23 percent quality actives that clean better and more efficiently and are safe to use. A lot more quality actives cost more but give the customer a better and safer cleaner that cleans a lot more per gallon than the 5 percent cleaner. As an example, it will take almost two 55-gallon drums of the 5 percent active aircraft cleaner to wash one C-130 military aircraft. Remember, the 5 percent cleaner is 95 percent water. In an actual demonstration of the *23 percent active* aircraft cleaner, *ten gallons did a better job.* The 5 percent cleaner was *used straight* out of the two drums. The 23 percent highly concentrated cleaner applied through a foam unit used less than ten gallons. You get what you pay for. *At this rate, two 55-gallon drums of your quality high solids (actives) will clean 11 C-130s to the one cleaned by the competitive low actives cleaner. Now, is our price too high?*

The lower price of the 5 percent cleaner was way over-priced for the value it didn't give. The quality cleaner was clearly worth the higher price in *labor savings* alone. The customer's lower price per gallon bought him 95 percent water, on which he probably paid shipping charges.

There is a way to show the difference in "actives" between the two industrial liquid cleaners. Measure one ounce of each cleaner into two beakers and boil away the water. The residue on each scale, by weight, is the actives or solids. The high quality cleaner left *23 percent by weight* of the one ounce of cleaner after boiling the water off. The lower priced cleaner left *5 percent by weight* out of one ounce of cleaner. *This "assumes" the solids of both cleaners are of the same quality, which they are not. Case closed!*

You must find out how your products compare to your competitors. Know the good ones and *know the cheats, like the dark dye, 5 percent guys,* who sell their low-priced, "highly-concentrated" junk everywhere. *If you know what the competition is selling, you can beat them every time.* This is *"street smart," big money selling!*

2. Discounting Strategy

Always remember you work hard for your money, *so don't give it away by discounting to get an order.* It will only *compound the future price increase negotiation* as you will not have any compromise room. If the customer is big and refuses a price increase or will not agree to the total amount of the increase, *you must have room in your profit margin to compromise on or "eat" the total increase to keep this major customer. Always sell your value added quality and service.* If you can figure something *other than giving away your commission and company profit* to close the prospect, do it. *Make discounting your very last resort. A giveaway is a one-time cost.* Lowering your price, say 5 percent, is 5 percent of your future income for however long you keep selling this customer. If your opening order is $1,000, 5 percent discount equals $50. If your commission is 10 percent, you now earn $95 or a loss of $5 times four orders per year equals $20 per year times ten years equals $200 times 100 plus customers equals *$20,000 you have given away* to your wealthy customers that your family could have used. Your company loses $50 on every $1,000 order. Fifty dollars times four orders per year, times ten years, times 100 customers and the company will have *lost $200,000.*

Sometimes a situation calls for you to offer a discount, and you have to do it to induce a *large prospect* to buy your company's products and services. In this situation, if you don't budge, and in your experience will lose the prospective customer, you must offer the lowest discount that you think will win the business—*then offer half of that.* You can always give a little more if you *start* low enough. If you are too stingy and always want it all, you will *not* end the year *No. 1 in sales or income.*

On the really big ones, ask your company for help. They know what their national account customers pay and what should be offered to be most likely to land your national prospect. The company may work out a *special commission package* for your work at bringing in the account and servicing its headquarters. *Use your company sales management as an excellent sales tool.* Prospects are flattered and impressed if the manufacturer's corporate sales and technical executives come to help negotiate and finalize the contract. Depending on the size of your company and the prospect company, the President of your company may come to meet the President of your new customer. It shows interest from the top and implies top service and appreciation for the business.

Know, inside and out, your company's *discount schedule* and how *it directly effects your commissions.* Always have *something else* other than giving away your commission dollars to offer as a *"closer."* Maybe, offer a piece of minor equipment or freight charge concession on the opening order. If necessary, come up with a *one-time* giveaway to get the order.

Remember, sell *quality* and *service! Throw away that discount crutch!*

3. How to Handle Price Increases

As costs of doing business continually go up, it becomes necessary for your company to announce a general price increase of say 5 percent across the board. *If this isn't handled carefully you and your company will lose some major customers* whose business was hard to get but you now enjoy.

Small and medium-sized customers will accept most price increases in stride. *Major customers are special* and must be handled individually and with care. Most companies give their customers advance notice of a price increase of at least 30 days. The sales representative needs extra time *to personally "sell"* his large sales volume customers on the upcoming price increase and of the company's need to raise prices. Some will thank you for the advance notice, and it should be more than 30 days for your big customers. Department stores won't get additional budget to cover the increase until the next season. So, they can't handle the increase in price until next season when they will include it in their budget. You will have to *sell your company* on going along with this delay, or stand to lose the customer. Your company will go along, unless management is not "Street Smart!" You and your company and your customer must agree on the timing and their OK before billing their next orders with the price increase. The computer must be programmed to implement the increase on the agreed date. *A professional sales representative not only has to sell the big ones but he has to know how to keep them.*

Some national customers will flatly refuse to accept an increase. Five percent to them is big dollars, and with many suitors in the wings just waiting for you to make a mistake, *your company will have to negotiate* a smaller increase or none at all. Depending on how strong your brand is and how strong and close you and your management are to this customer, a compromise will be worked out.

It is suicide for any company to just think of themselves and force a price increase on all their customers, regardless of size or situation. I have seen this first hand and major customers were lost, some after 30 years of profitable and excellent business relationships. Why would any company do this? You guessed it! The company was sold! New owners didn't understand or care about past working relationships. *They wanted bigger profits now*, so every customer was told they were getting a set price increase. If a salesman was too *"chicken"* to raise his biggest customers the full amount, the difference will be taken out of the salesman's commissions. *The new owners raised everybody substantially and lost most of the big customers.* They got more money out of fewer customers. They could have had most of the increase dollars and still kept their biggest customers, *but they weren't "street smart!"* Thankfully, this is a rare situation.

4. Bid Strategy and Other Considerations

Bids worth bidding are usually very big volume dollars in sales and, because you have to cut the price, the commission rate must also be cut. Commission dollars are still substantial because of the high volume.

Some large corporations don't get involved in bidding because of the very low prices required to win a bid. The government is partial to minority and women-owned companies by law, which raises the odds of winning a bid for all the others. Other than this, there are many companies that make their living from the bid system, mostly in government. To be successful and have a decent chance to win, the product quality must by necessity be cut back enough to meet the minimum bid requirements so you can cut costs and realize some reasonable profit if you happen to win the bid.

A corporation or company with quality products can't compete. Even if you cut your list price to 10 percent *above cost,* you will lose the bid. If by a miracle you won the bid, what are you going to do on next year's bid? Go to a 5 percent profit? Most companies aren't prepared or willing to sell their *quality products at this low price or profit level* and it is still extremely doubtful the bid would be won, *even at 5 percent above cost.* You're bidding against professional *"bottom-feeders"* that make their living on bid business.

I once lost a military bid, even though I came in with the lowest price which I found out after the fact, when I went in to look at where I came out in the bid process. When I tried to find out why I lost to a price higher than mine, I was told that after figuring in the difference in *payment terms,* my price was actually second lowest. My company's payment terms were "Net 30 days" and the rival bidder's terms were "2 percent, 10 days, net 30." In other words, we required payment within thirty days. The winning bidder with a higher bid price offered a 2 percent discount if paid in ten days or the total was due in 30 days, the same as my bid. Now this is the *baloney* you must contend with in a bid situation as the military *never paid anything in ten days* and most probably most invoices go to ninety days or more before payment is actually made. This other company knew this and put the 2 percent in their terms to give them a slight advantage. They knew they would never have to give the 2 percent discount and the military knew they would not ever be able to take advantage of this 2 percent, but figured it in lowering that company's bid by 2 percent, and awarded the contract to them.

Dilbert ©: Scott Adams/Dist. by United Feature Syndicate, Inc.

The bidder usually must travel to the place that awards the bid, where the bids are opened, and look at the last bid results *to guess* how to bid the next bid. All other bidders do the same. *It is a chess game with a blindfold* to estimate how low all the other bidders will bid their product or products. Professional bidders get to know their competitors and the way they are likely to bid. *A bidder's product must meet the bid specifications, sometimes written with the help of one of the bidders, in such a way as to specify a feature only their product has.*

I was bidding on a US Navy order for 30,000 aerosol cans of a solvent degreaser. I knew the company and people that I was bidding against and had lost to them before, but it was always close. On the last bid I lost I had pulled out all the stops and instructed our aerosol supplier to remove the cardboard case dividers and to replace the metal caps with plastic to cut our cost and bid price to the bone. Our aerosol supplier was located in Chicago and the freight was killing me as the shipping point was California. My competitor was located in California too and must have the same costs to consider in their bids, but they were consistently beating my almost at cost bid. I discussed my bidding situation with my West Coast chemist and plant manager, Dick Miller, who told me he would do some detective work.

Just before all bids were due, Dick called me and said: "Do you want to beat them by a mile on this bid or lower your price just enough to win? What the hell are you talking about I'm down to my shorts now! I can't go any lower! Dick laughed and told me he had made a few calls and found the West Coast aerosol packager that was supplying my competitor and who would now be glad to supply us too. Dick swore them to secrecy. We now had the advantage of the substantial freight savings to work with in bidding for the 30,000 aerosol cans. I knew how my competitor had bid and the amount of their last bid. I bid a prudent amount lower than I knew they would. When I arrived home the night the bids were to be opened, this competitor had called my home and left a message saying, "touché! You won the bid, but at that price you had to give up all your commission! We know you can't go any lower than that so we'll win the next bid!" Little did they know that I had a bright bidding future, at least until they find out how I could keep bidding "below cost."

Finally, as a salesman, *you want all the volume you can possibly get this year*, and let the chips fall where they may. You may end the year with the highest volume of sales in your company, but not the highest commission. The company's profit and your commissions were cut to the bone. That may be great to be the *king of the hill this year*, but all your competitors will see your bid price and come in next year much lower than you can. Even though you point to the previous year's bid figures, *your sales decrease will be so big you may even lose your good job*. Is this the reward for going through all this trouble? *Yes!* In this book I am talking to *first-class professional salesmen*. You represent quality companies and corporations who manufacture quality products and offer quality service. *My advice is to forget the bid business*. Your company may have a military specialist to handle all government bids.

I must make a proviso to the above so you don't give up on military or government business altogether. In some cases, such as was true at that time, navy aircraft carriers did not go out for bid on their flight deck and hangar deck cleaner. It was left up to the "Air Department" officers on board ship to decide, after some testing, which flight deck cleaner they preferred. They would tell the navy procurement department to order the amount of material needed and give them the price. (That opportunity is now gone as the navy has an approved vendor list who must now bid on this business.)

There are still situations with government where federal, state, county, city and military business is granted *outside of the bid process* in "special cases," but I suggest unless you already know someone or know about a special situation, your time will be much better spent on your traditional prospects.

4

Keys to the Treasure Chest

1. 'There are Only Trees and Rocks up There'

"You had no business selling what you sold up there! There are only trees and rocks up there!" These were the words spoken to me at a meeting in San Francisco by Mr. Louis Brunner, President and founder of The Brulin Company.

I thanked Mr. Brunner and reminded him that behind one big rock was a sprawling complex in Santa Rosa of the Hewlett-Packard Co.

I am telling this story to illustrate the *power* of a *burning desire, competitiveness, hard work, determination, product knowledge and salesmanship.* For many years the territory north of the Golden Gate Bridge was "covered" by the "Bay Area" salesmen, both of whom were "Master Salesmen." From the sales generated north of the "Golden Gate Bridge" and north of Sacramento, it is apparent that this vast area of redwood trees, rivers, mountains and the "wine country" was not covered except on vacations. We finally hired a local person to cover the "trees and rocks" north of the "bridge." The best that was accomplished in this territory all this time was to generate $6,000 in commissions per year.

After five years as an assistant national sales manager, which meant I did the traveling and my recent marriage to a Northern California girl, I arranged to take over the "trees and rocks" territory. Everyone thought I was out of my mind, including Louis Brunner, President. It would be the end of my sales career and it was like I banished myself to Siberia. I left a good paying sales management job for the worst territory in the country. In my position I could have chosen a major market territory almost anywhere in the United States. Why would I do such a stupid thing? My wife of one year was born and raised in Eureka, CA!

From five years as a national sales manager I had 110 percent *product knowledge*. I had a *"burning desire"* to show everybody I wasn't crazy. I was *determined* and *confident and extremely competitive*. I worked hard, and it was hard, but nothing could stop me as I knew my products inside and out. I knew what every product could do and was willing no, *eager* to demonstrate, put my enthusiasm on stage, close the order and take a customer away from a competitor. To my advantage, I was there working for the customers while my competitors would make their "country run" once or twice a year. As I took their customers, there was very little reason for them to take a drive into the country.

In the ten years I was responsible for sales in my territory I was in the "Top Ten" in the country in sales every month and several times I sold more in a month than everyone else and was No. 1. It is remarkable to me that I could sell more dollars than a major market salesman in New York, Boston, Chicago, Minneapolis, Los Angeles, San Francisco, Seattle, Miami, Atlanta and Dallas.

Using the principles and secrets told in this book, I sold this "only trees and rocks" territory from $6,000 to $80,000 in commissions. (Approximately $140,000 in today's dollars) If you care enough to look, there is business behind every rock that your competitors don't see. Enjoy the book and all the new found money you will earn.

2. How to be No. 1 in Sales and Income

First, you must master the basics. Learn everything about your products, pricing and discount policies. Keep detailed records. Learn why your products are better than your competitors. Make the decision to go all-out to be No. 1. You must have the *burning desire to be No. 1.* That attitude will carry you through the tough times, which every salesman must overcome and continue to press on. Nothing can stop you from your goal. Here is where you will leave some of your competitors behind. No matter what happens, keep moving ahead with full confidence as you have the best product in the world. It is your mission and responsibility to introduce the benefits of your product to all the companies in your territory who have been uninformed that there is a superior product they should be using. Armed with knowledge, desire and confidence, you are ready to employ some common sense tactics to get ahead of your formidable competitors for top sales increase in your company.

1. Set a long-term goal that, from where you sit right now, looks impossible to achieve, but will insure that you end the year No. 1.

2. Divide that goal by 12 months which gives you the number you must achieve or exceed every month.

3.   Divide each month by 20 days that will give you the dollars you must sell or exceed every working day.

   You are now ahead of most of your peers. Now plan exactly how you will achieve this daily sales goal. How will you cover your territory to maximize your time in front of your prospects and customers and not in your car? Prioritize your valuable time. Turn off your car radio and think about your next call.

   If you find yourself falling behind your plan, *cheat*. If you do the unthinkable, you can find at least an extra month's selling time.

1.   Start extra early every workday to arrive at your first call when the first shift begins, usually 7:00 am. Most salesmen, for various reasons, don't consistently make their first sales presentation at 7:00 am. So if you do, you are ahead in number of sales presentations at the end of the year. This early start, at one hour per day head start, will give you an advantage of about 240 bonus hours more than your fellow salesmen.

2.   Extend the normal sales day. Force yourself to stay in the territory an extra hour every day and make just one more sales presentation. Most outside sales reps won't do this consistently. This discipline will give you another 200+ hours toward your goal that others will dismiss with excuses.

3.   Pick several hours each weekend to plan and prioritize your next week's sales plan. Make it a regular time that your family respects every weekend. This will give you about 100 planning hours and you will never have to wonder which way to go on Monday morning.

4.   How do you win, over all your competition? You have to put in the time! If you want to be No. 1 badly enough to put in the extra time, you will give yourself approximately 540 extra hours toward your success in a year. Dividing eight hours per work day into 540 hours equals 67.5 days or an extra two months and one week of selling more than your competitors in a year's time. If this were a horse race, which it is, you would be out in front and will win.

Photo printed with permission of the Riverside County Economic
Development Agency

3. All of Us Are the Same, Except for One Thing

Everyone in sales has a head with a brain, two arms, two legs, a body, an education, a vehicle and a product. Everyone starts out with about the same equipment. Who then, will win, and how?

The person who wants to win the most! The winning salesman will take these similar basics and work them faster, smarter and harder than the others with the same equipment. The winning salesman arose above all the other salesmen with the same basic equipment by his or her *burning desire* to win. This salesman won't be distracted or stopped for any reason. This salesman has the competitiveness, desire and motivation to be No. 1, and with the same tools at this salesman's disposal organizes, plans and makes more sales calls than all the others. The more calls this salesman makes, the more confidence he or she gets and even more and bigger sales are "closed." This encourages this salesman to do more planning and make even more successful sales calls. This salesman has left all the others, with the same equipment and potential, way behind because they lacked the "burning desire" to plan and do everything necessary that it takes, such as hard work, to become a successful professional salesman.

The less time a salesman, without a plan, invests in his success, the less confident and more defensive he becomes and the more sales he loses. It's a downward spiral. A salesman must go all out, all the time, and fully use all the tools he was given if he has any chance to succeed, not to mention coming out at year end the No. 1 salesman in sales and earnings in his corporation.. If a salesman has doubts about himself or his products, he needs to get his attitude and confidence straightened out fast or choose another profession. Remember, salesmanship is a profession that is *learned*, so learn it fast and enjoy your rewards, which are many not the least of which is money. Every salesman has the tools but the key to winning is *desire*. End of story.

4. Which Came First, the Chicken or the Egg

In salesmen's terms, which comes first, motivation or desire? Most salesmen would like to be No. 1, but for many, all that is necessary to achieve it takes too much time and sacrifice, and they don't need the hassle as they think they make a good living now with ease. These salesmen really don't have the "desire" or the "motivation." Different things motivate each person. If, in January, a corporation offered as motivation a new vehicle to the salesman who had the biggest dollar increase in sales at the end of the year, most will be motivated to try. Their wives and children will motivate them out the door every morning. Some salesmen, who have dropped behind, will lose their *motivation*, as they believe there is no hope. Their desire is still there, but their motivation to continue going all out for a "hopeless cause" is gone. So, it seems *desire* first and *motivation* second. Who cares? Does "desire" give you the motivation to succeed or does the "motivation" of something you desire give you what it takes for you to do your utmost best selling job consistently all year? The *burning desire* for something you desperately want gives a salesman the *motivation* to accomplish an outstanding selling effort.

You have to keep yourself *motivated* all throughout the year. How? Go to a new car dealership and look at the car inside and out that is the first prize. See if they have your or your wife's favorite color. Sit in the driver's seat. Breathe in the "new car smell." Pick up a brochure and tear out the page of the car you want and tape it to your dashboard to keep you motivated. Even if there are salesmen ahead of you at various times of the year, you are still in the race and you still have a few big prospects you expect to close. Keep *motivated* to keep going even smarter. You intend to win, but even if the fickle finger of fate smiles on someone else in the end, you realize if you keep the pressure on yourself, you will have earned enough extra money with your big sales increase dollars, to buy the damn car yourself. Desire makes you want to, and *motivation* gets you to your goal. So, which comes first? Neither, *desire* nor *motivation* can function without the other, so it is ruled a "tie" as they come in together, hand in hand. You need them both to succeed and attain your goal. If you have a *burning desire*, you have already found your motivation. Competitiveness is motivation enough for some!

5. How to Become Street Smart

A brand new salesman who has never sold a product or service before is not yet "street smart." He has completed college, the corporate product knowledge school and practiced giving and critiquing role-playing of simulated prospect sales calls. He is still not "street smart." He is now a well-educated, well-coached robot sent out to preach the corporate gospel to a multitude of non-believers.

What, then, is being *"Street Smart?"* Selling experience in the real world! A salesman who adjusts to his customer and prospect reactions to his presentations is becoming "street smart." Learning what his competitors are selling and how it compares to his product and service. Learning to sell to fill the *"buyer's needs"* and desires rather than your desires. Being *confident* and a good amount of successful field experience and *marketplace awareness* is the basis for being "street smart." Street smarts come to the professional salesman with experience. Street smarts are necessary to beat your competitors. Being "street smart" is learning everything that is going on in your marketplace. "Street smart" means competitiveness, determination, being inquisitive, using common sense and the *burning desire* to win. It means you are in the fight and have figured out how to win and are winning. Being "street smart" usually means a salesman is a veteran of the market share wars. Being "street smart" is sensing the correct presentation to motivate a buyer to buy in his marketplace. A "street smart" salesman knows what it takes to win. *It pays off big to become "Street Smart."* Every chapter in this book tells you how to become successful and "Street Smart!" Why "Street Smart?" *Because, being "Street Smart" "Shows You The Money!"*

5

Prepare For Battle

1. Competitive Spirit

Pete Carroll, who has won two national championships in the last three years and was a couple seconds from winning a third as head football coach at The University of Southern California ("USC"), said: "The No.1 thing we look for is how *competitive* they are; that will take you past speed. Just to get guys that can run is not enough."

Be competitive! It's your territory! All the business belongs to you. All you have to do is go out there and get it. America was built on the competitive system, in sports and in business. Go out aggressively and discourage your competition. Take over your territory. You and your products and service are the best! In my experience competitiveness can not be taught. You either have it or you don't.

In sports, you study the other team's game film to learn how to beat them. You learn their weaknesses and their tactics so you can adjust and beat them. If you are a competitive salesman, you want to find out all you can about the other competitive teams operating in your territory so you can tailor your presentation to offer more than they do. Make them an offer they can't refuse. You know they can't refuse because you know for certain your offer is better because you did your homework.

The more business you take from your competitors, the more discouraged they will get. Some will try to find out what you are doing to get their former customer's business. Some won't bother. If they lose enough customers, they will also lose their jobs. One, maybe, might have the same competitive zeal that you do, and then the battle is on. The customer should be asked, "Why didn't this other guy, if he had your interests at heart, give you this new deal in the first place?" Whoever is the most fiercely competitive will probably win overall, but the other competitive guy won't let you have all the business because he is competitive too. The two of you will own the territory, each wishing the other guy was never born. That's competition! Competitiveness is a positive motivating force that drives a salesman or athlete to win any and all contests and never give up.

2. Competition

Make a point of learning as much information as you can about your competition. If you are selling apparel to major department stores, you know all the other lines the department you sell carries and you can see their products. You can ask the buyer why she buys some of the other brands and how they stack up in sales with your brand. They might not tell you, but you can ask. Each department has a fixed dollar amount of "open-to-buy." You must beat your biggest competitors to present your new line first, when the buyer has all of next season's open-to-buy dollars. If the buyer has been sold extra promotions and hot close-out deals by your top competitors before you make your presentation, the buyer may like your line and promotions, but won't have any money left. You get there first and let your competitors find out the buyer is out of money! At *New York Market*, if you are entertaining your top account, your competition isn't, and vice versa.

Write your competitors on your account sheet for each account and you will begin to see a picture of who, where and why about your competitors. *What you don't know will hurt you.* How could generals fight a war if they didn't know who they were fighting, their enemy's strength and positions? *General Robert E. Lee* in the Civil War, having graduated from West Point, knew the Union *General George Meade* who had just been appointed by *President Abraham Lincoln* to lead the "Army of the Potomac" against him. General Lee knew his competitor, Meade, would be slow to get organized and that gave Lee a strategic advantage in consolidating his positions for the coming *"Battle of Gettysburg."* But Lee was "blind" and *had no other intelligence* from his "eyes," the cavalry, leading raids in a different area. So, without knowledge of his competitor's whereabouts, Lee eventually was forced by events and *lack of knowledge* to fight as an attacker against well fortified Union positions, and *lost the battle and eventually the war. Know your competitor*, his strengths and weaknesses, and his products and how they stack up against your products, *so you can win your battles and the war.*

In the *Battle of Midway*, the United States won the battle because we broke the Japanese code and *knew when and where they would strike* and were waiting for them. *If you ignore your competition, you just might lose the war.*

Learn all you can about your competition, *but*, for your own good *do not "bad mouth" your competition.* It will come back to haunt you.

Remember, if you *help your contact person* better his or her position with your products and knowledge *more than your competitors, you will win.* Liking a competitive sales representative personally *will take second place to the buyer's self-interest.* It helps if you are liked, too.

3. Competition From Within Your Own Company

Most salesmen don't realize this, and some never will that you should always treat the employees of your own company as you would treat a customer. A chorus of negatives from your co-workers can eventually sink your ship. A positive relationship with your co-workers is much more effective in support of you and your customers. You are competing with other salesmen in your corporation for the fastest possible service to your customers. Who do you think might get first consideration to get shipment of a scarce product that only a few sales representatives can get? "The squeaky wheel always gets the grease" might be OK on a wagon train, but on a corporate team the rep who screams his demands and "talks down" to his co-workers gets "greased" with slow order filling and complaints to his sales management. Complaints add up to the point that if one good customer complains to the company about the salesman's "squeaky wheel," he will be gone.

It is much better to enjoy the company, your co-workers and your job and to make friends rather than to build enemies within *your work family.* It makes for a much better life and work environment. *It has a direct affect on your sales attitude which must remain positive.* So, count to ten, and always be considerate of your co-workers. "You will get more with honey, than with vinegar!"

4. The Sales Conference

Bob Felgen, second seated row, fourth from right (with white badge)

The annual sales conference, which is sometimes held at a resort with golf and other outings planned after the business sessions, is a time for the sales representative to learn, interact with his peers and enjoy himself. The pressure and stress of a salesman's territory responsibilities and his family obligations are temporarily lifted from his shoulders. It's time to let off steam! This makes some salesmen lose their senses. *Wrong!* Most salesmen don't realize they are being "sized-up" and judged for potential future promotion into sales management. If the No. 1 salesman at the time of the conference acts improperly, he will not, most likely, be invited to join the executive sales management team. *"He is a good salesman, but not management material!"*

A salesman can be very conscientious all year in his territory and conduct himself and his business professionally. Then comes the annual or semi-annual sales conference and he now *thinks he is on vacation.* He goes out with "the boys" in the evening, drinks too much, gets back late and gets little sleep. The next day he sleeps through the company breakfast and he and his bloodshot eyes and throbbing head drags himself to his seat as far back as possible. He looks awful. He has trouble keeping his eyes open during the presentations. *All of this didn't go unnoticed* by the sales manager and other top management, which gave them a *negative opinion of his judgment, work ethic and character.* He has lowered his good standing with his bosses and other corporate executives. He doesn't act this way at home or in his territory, *but there is something about a sales conference!*

At your sales conference, act like the gentleman you are, don't drink too much, or *better yet, not at all,* get plenty of sleep so you will be alert and *participate in the meetings* and always remember, *"Big brother is watching you"!*

6

What Do You Want Most of All

1. Veteran Salesmen, Something to Think About

We have a lot of business and have worked hard to get it. We are up there with the top salesmen in our corporation and feel comfortable that we are at the top of our sales profession. We all know our competitors. They aren't rolling in the gutter. In fact, some of them look mighty prosperous driving around our territory in those big cars with smiles on their faces. We also have big cars and occasionally smile too. So what! What's your point, there's enough for everybody.

If we happened to find out that a newer salesman, in a small market, was making twice the commissions we were earning and shipping more too, we would be very upset, to say the least. How can this be? We top salesmen are in the major markets of the country. How can he or she earn twice as much as we do? And, he drives a pick-up truck! The new guy has dominated his market and gets nearly all the business to be had. His competitors packed up and moved out. We, on the other hand, are content to share our territories with other competitors who we know and with whom we are content to co-exist.

If we top salesmen could go up in a space shuttle to the International Space Station and look down on our territories with different colored laser beams *showing our customers and our competitor's customers*, we probably would jump or never come down.

International Space Station image courtesy of NASA

It would knock us off our comfortable TV chair if we knew how much *money* our competitors are pulling out of *our territory!* Just think of how much of our money our competitors are sucking out of our wallets, affecting our family's well being, investments for the future, the new car we want and a bigger house for our family.

We wouldn't stand for someone stealing money from our families. That is just what is happening.

We top salesmen had better wake up from our complacency and go out and take back all that money that is being siphoned off from our territories. If each of us has three or four high income competitors in his territory, each earning approximately the same as we are, our potential increase in income is three or four times what we are now earning. Now, that is worth the extra effort to earn back our own money, which some other family has been enjoying, on our tab. Why have we been calling these rascals "friends?" Call it like it is: *enemies!* We are letting them steal from our families! Let's show them these territories belong to us. In my territory, all the business should be mine, and I'm going after all of it. My family's money is out there for the taking. I better plan my attack. Nothing can stop me. If I thought I was on top, I wasn't. I hope my competitors don't read this book!

2. Motivation

To keep yourself *motivated* all the time, have your week pre-planned so you know where you are going and why. Have everything ready for those sales calls. On the weekend, write out your daily call plan in your weekly planner and check them off as you finish each call, making notes on your customer or prospect account sheet to help you on your next sales call to the facility. Order anything you may have promised to do, *now!* Make appointments ahead where necessary to make your calls more positive and efficient. If an emergency comes up at one of your customers not on your list for this week, you will have to break away from your plan if the situation can't be handled by a few phone calls from your car. After the emergency is handled, go back and do the best you can to finish the day's schedule. Possibly the two or three calls you missed could be added, one per day, to the rest of the week. Also, be sure customers with whom you had appointments that day are called at once to be rescheduled.

What has this to do with motivation? Have you ever wandered around on any morning wondering whom to call on and then driving to a friendly customer for coffee and a possible small fill-in order? We all have, I am afraid. This from a lack of organization and planning and it's discouraging, not motivating! *Isn't it more of a motivation to know, all the time, every day, where you are going?* You will be more successful which motivates you to do even more. *"Success breeds success"* is true. If you are in a race and are way behind, you lose your motivation to keep going. If you are out in front, don't we all want to work even harder to stay in front and *discourage* everyone from catching us? *So, consistent extra effort to plan ahead keeps you highly motivated.* If you can keep yourself motivated, you will win the race.

If you know you need occasionally to be re-motivated, write something on the back of a calling card and *scotch tape the motivation to your dashboard* where you can see it every time you drive your car to the next call. Something like, "You are No. 1. Keep going!" "Keep Smiling!" "Close the sale!" "Sell the *benefits* dummy!" "Make that *extra* call!" "Don't *waste time!*" "Ask questions and *listen.* "A slip of the lip can sink a ship!" "Fulfill all my promises *at once.*" "Don't drive by the *"mother load!"* "Turn off the radio." "You are prospecting for *gold!*" You will have your own reminders that will keep reminding you to stay on the right track and when you have learned to do it without being reminded, take that note off the dash and throw it away. Better yet, keep it in the glove box to be put back if you need reminding from time to time. Why are you working so hard? Whatever *motivates* you to sell like hell should be put on the dash so it will motivate you every day, all the time. Don't forget to remove the cards when you take a prospect or customer to lunch. "Write 'til they bleed" won't go over very well! Always keep your chin up, hold your head up high, look at the bright side of everything, always be positive, be confident, keep smiling and the world will smile back and keep you motivated. Just visualize a *gold bar* behind every door and you will find a way to get through the door!

Image courtesy of www.sidereus.org/MONEY
The Sidereus Foundation is a member of the Starfields Network
www.Starfields.net

Through the years every account you open will generate enough commission to buy even more *gold bars*, some more than others, but *gold bars* just the same! How many *gold bars* will you earn?

3. More on Sales Managers and Motivation

There is something I have observed through the years about motivation. The primary job of a Sales Manager is to motivate their salesmen to always do their best. Like Knute Rockne of Notre Dame, Vince Lombardi, the winning Super Bowl coach of the Green Bay Packers, and Pete Carroll, Head Football Coach of The University of Southern California, who *motivated* and *inspired* their teams to win. Their players wanted to win. They were *motivated to play way beyond their normal capabilities.*

Sales Managers must encourage all their salesmen to perform way above their normal limits. His constant *encouragement* keeps his salesmen believing in themselves and with this *confidence* they are *motivated to excel* to the top of their potential. The most valuable Sales Manager to his corporation is the one that *motivates* his salesmen with *encouragement* and who *leads by example*.

On the other hand, I am sorry to say, there are some sales managers who are always negative, insensitive and highly critical. Salesman's errors should be pointed out with some tact so they can improve. Some Sales Managers misuse their authority and *"manage with a whip."* Most salesmen are confident and proud of their sales ability and respond to these "prison guards in a suit" like a stubborn mule and won't budge an inch or cooperate with them. This is reverse motivation! There is some short-term benefit derived from the negative feelings generated by the sales manager's harsh anti-motivational behavior. The strong salesmen will work harder to stick it to the "Sales Mangler" and make him eat his criticism. Trouble is it motivates the salesman with a burning desire borne of hatred to achieve much higher sales which helps the "bad" Sales Manager and the corporation. It always amazed me that top management treats the "bad" sales managers like customers, they are "always right!" These sales managers might have been good salesmen at one time but don't know how to properly handle the authority they were given. Most good professional salesmen provide their own motivation and goals and possess the *self confidence* to keep going and never give up or let themselves be discouraged by anything or anyone.

DILBERT© reprinted by permission of United Feature Syndicate, Inc.

The best salesmen work around, and are successful in spite of, the negative sales manager. The good salesmen do not need a negative sales manager. This type of sales manager creates a negative charge! The great sales manager that *moti-*

vates and *leads by example* creates a *positive charge of enthusiasm and confidence* all around him and his salesmen perform far beyond their normal capability. The great sales manager creates a much better and healthier culture *in which to excel,* and enjoy it too.

7

From Zero to Gold

1. Get Organized!

To be organized, you must plan ahead. Order samples well in advance of a demonstration. Have plenty of order pads on hand. Set up files for all customers. Make or set up customer record sheets to carry with you in the car. Have extra sheets at home and in the car for prospect information. Have a box or case in the car or trunk with your sales supplies and literature. Order more literature, order pads and samples well before you run out. Keep extra pens in the glove compartment. Fill your car with gasoline on the weekend and change oil on the weekend too. Stock a cooler with water or soda on ice so you don't lose time stopping during selling hours. In other words, think of every thing you will need to support your selling success and then make sure you take the time to order these necessary supplies in advance.

This avoids having to promise to send literature to a prospect which cools the prospect and you won't be there to go over the fine points. It will probably go into the "round file" under the desk. When you are *organized*, you will always have all your selling tools when you go into battle. Selling something to someone who doesn't know you or your product is hard enough as it is, and even harder, if not impossible, without all your sales tools. Being organized is one of the requirements for becoming a professional salesman; the same as a gun and ammunition is a requirement of a soldier going into battle.

2. Planning For Success

What if "D-Day" was not planned? It's no different in selling. The salesman that does not plan how best to cover his territory, will lose the war and his selling job. A salesman who doesn't plan as well or consistently as his competitors will lose the war. A salesman can never reach the No. 1 status within his company if he is weak, inefficient and lazy about planning every week's and every day's sales calls. *Where you go and when is the key to your success.* Timing is everything! There must be a well thought-out reason for a salesman to make every call at a certain time. A salesman's time is very valuable and should not be wasted by wandering around wondering whom to call on.

3. Set High Goals

Set realistic, high sales goals to achieve. Then plan on how best to achieve those goals. First, break down the final goal into months, weeks and days. Now, what do you have to do every day to achieve this goal? Some days will fall short of your plan and some will be over plan. Don't let yourself be discouraged on a down day. Even the down sales days contribute something toward the good sales days, so keep looking up and always keep your positive attitude. Keep moving forward positively toward your goal. Let your competitors get discouraged. They have the same problems that you have, but some don't have any goal and most let them selves be discouraged. You have the distinct advantage because you have a *goal* and know where you are going and how to get there. Just keep going positively and consistently toward your goal and you will reach it.

8

A Priority Matter

1. Prioritizing Your Time

All companies, sales managers and you want the biggest sales increase possible. You want to be *number one* in your company in *sales and income* and so does everyone else. Let's plan a strategy. The two obvious ways to get an increase is to sell your current customers more and sell new customers. There is only so much time in a day, so where should we spend it? Selling your customers more is, or should be, easier because they are already buying from you and your company. You look around or ask what your customer is buying from someone else an item or items that your company manufactures. Then you tell them why they should buy those items from your company, such as a quantity discount, fewer invoices to process and fewer sales reps to take up your valuable time. So, you are able to get an item or two in. This is good and a sales rep should try to do this with every current customer. We tend to spend too much time with the people that we know and like, which is natural—a port in the storm. Consider this in planning how to give away your valuable time. If the average customer buys $10,000 a year, and you sell an additional item in the amount of $1,000, you have a 10 percent increase. This is good.

This 10 percent increase took a certain amount of your time. If this same amount of time was used to land a new account with a $1,000 order, this and all subsequent orders that year equal a 100 percent sales and commission increase. So, your big money increases are to be found in *new accounts*. You have 100 or so customers that require service of various degrees. To be a success in your sales profession, *spend most of your time prospecting* and presenting to non-customers. *New customer dollars are all 100 percent increase*. You can easily see that making your rounds and calling on all your customers once a month or every six weeks without fail chasing fill-ins and new items won't earn you or your company much of an increase, if any. Do you spend any personal time with a $100, $200 or $300 customer when you are growing a million dollar territory? No. Those small customers are costing you money. They are too small to warrant your professional time. Service your large accounts enough to keep them and grow them and use the rest of your time to prospect new accounts and their 100 percent increase. The name of the game for a professional sales representative and all companies and corporations, is *sales increase!* Your reputation is made with *sales increase* numbers. Your *income and bonus money* are earned with *sales increase dollars. New accounts* are where you must force yourself to spend about 75 percent of your valuable time. Lawyers charge $300 per hour. Accountants charge $250 per hour. Can you earn that in the hour you spend with a customer? You can and more, by steadily selling new customers. *New business is where the big money is!*

2. Other Time Considerations

Optimizing your efficiency during *"prime selling time"* between 7:00 am and 4:00 pm is a vital strategy in striving to be "No. 1." If you plan your week and every day ahead of time in non-prime time, you will maximize your prime selling time presentations and sales. Most sales representatives are inefficient in their use of their *prime selling time* and end the year in the middle of the "average" pack.

Think of the prime time of your selling day as a *minefield full of distractions.* You must be aware of these distractions or they will blow up your chance of *being No. 1 and getting to the big money.* There are all kinds of distractions, which are veiled excuses to avoid making the number of presentations as planned.

1. Too much driving time between presentations. Plan better.

2. Long lunches by yourself or with customers.

3. Too many time-outs for coffee.

4. Family distractions from your prime selling window—dropping off and/or picking up the kids to or from school, soccer, or dance lessons to help out your spouse. A spouse has to be reminded that if you worked at an office job, they would have to make other arrangements, except in an emergency. The family has to be informed that a sales representative's prime selling time has to be respected for the good of the family's welfare.

5. Car repairs. A car is the sales rep's office and should be kept in good repair and good clean appearance during non-prime selling time.

6. "Mister Mom." When both parents work, they each have to respect and support each other's job. Both have to help out at home as a team for the good of the family. If the family has children, grandparents might take them during the day or some other suitable day-care/teaching program to enable both parents to give full-time concentration to success in their careers.

7. Getting discouraged and knocking-off early to reward ourselves with pie and coffee. "When the going gets tough," which it will, "the tough will keep going." There will be some of those days, and you're human, so go have that pie and coffee, but don't make it a bad habit.

8. Neglecting parking tickets so you have to take time off to go to court. Take care of your personal finances so you can concentrate on your selling with confidence.

9. *Divorce.* Your prime-time selling time just hit a mine and blew up. You have to survive, and you will, and just keep going and become fully aware that your job is your very best friend. Sales professionals have to be strong and will push forward and be successful no matter what happens. It's not the end of the world! Keep selling and at the end of the year you will probably be better off than before.

10. There are many more distractions to throw you off course every day. Know where you want to go every day and don't let anyone or any thing waste your prime selling time plans. (Unless a major customer needs help *now!*)

3. Appointments

Making appointments is a courtesy to the customer or prospect and will save you precious time. By planning ahead, you know where you will be next week, so make your appointments this week. Try to steer your appointments to the days you will be covering certain areas or towns. If covering a big city, try to be in a different area each day. By calling the week before their appointment book is full, you can request the appointment for the day you plan to be in that area. It doesn't always work out the way you plan, but it will save you time and get you *more sales presentations per day*, as most will honor your request.

If you go in cold without an appointment, your percent chances of being able to make a presentation are slim to none and you waste valuable time. You also might come in at an inopportune time when the last thing the buyer wants to see is a salesman. You avoid being the salesman the busy and upset buyer doesn't want to see. *Let a competitor drop in unannounced* and bear the brunt of the buyer's fury. You make an appointment and you can look forward to a more pleasant discussion of your products. If something came up unexpectedly, and the buyer can't see you, the situation will be told to you in a civil and apologetic manner and with your credibility in tact for the next appointment.

You have the best chance of getting an appointment with your major prospects and customers when you want them, the longer the time before the appointment. You know where you will be all this month as you have a plan. Why wait until the last week or last minute to call for your appointment? Start reserving your appointment times and dates early, when it is the most efficient to your travel plan. The earlier you make your appointments, the chances of you getting the time and date you want is nearer to 100 percent.

Always be on time for your appointments and make the time interesting and beneficial to the customer or prospect. Be sensitive to their valuable time, too. Do not overstay your welcome and then your next appointment will be easier to get.

4. Entertainment

Entertainment should not be necessary if you offer good value and service. This is true, but in the real world some persons with the authority to buy your products like being entertained. It makes them feel important and it is justified in their own mind as their due or legitimate repayment for giving the business to you and your company. In this environment, if your arch-competitor starts entertaining more often or more lavishly, you will lose this account anyway. At first, this buyer will play both vendors against each other giving some of your business to the other guy. He likes the increased attention and entertainment. One of the two vendors will reach a point of no return and stop entertaining this person and this will end his business. There is no long-term business in this situation.

Before you start entertaining, think twice, then think again, because *once you start, it is almost impossible to stop.* You can beg off in some circumstances, but you're hooked for the duration of your business life with this customer once you start. They expect you to take them to lunch every time you make an appointment with them. Sure, you get an order, but a big chunk of your *prime time selling hours* are gone.

If your customer orders alcohol drinks while you are entertaining him at lunch, you cannot join in as you have to make more calls and drive that afternoon. Politely give your reasons and order a non-alcoholic drink. If you are coerced into it by an important customer or prospect, you should not make any more calls that afternoon and hopefully realize this is the last time, or *making No. 1 and the big money will not be a reasonable possibility,* if you make it home after lunch. Depending on the situation, *I recommend establishing right from the start that you don't drink at lunch* as your company policy forbids it and the fact that you must drive and see other customers that same afternoon. I know of an instance where a major customer called the company to say their sales representative called on them with the smell of alcohol on his breath and didn't want him to service their account anymore. This was a veteran salesman and a major national account. Those were expensive drinks!

So, do not start entertaining unless you determine it is absolutely necessary to get or keep business. It's not so much the cost, but *the prime selling time lost forever.* Do it if you feel it is appropriate in the evening as a thank you for something big that happened pertaining to business, such as finally landing a big customer after a long period of heavy negotiations by both sides.

Imagine how much time will be lost over a year's time if a salesman is in the bad habit of taking several customers to lunch each time he works with them?

Some companies and big corporations encourage their salaried sales representatives to entertain customers as a sales tool to get and keep more business. They even have a Human Resources performance review question asking how many customers you entertained at a dinner or major sporting event. In these cases, you must entertain, on your own time, at least the number of times indicated on the review form. These corporations have "corporate boxes" where they play host to customers at major sporting events. The sales reps are expected to entertain their biggest customers and prospects. All entertainment expenses are covered on the salesman's expense account. The salesman is expected to use up his annual entertainment budget or he is not considered by his sales manager to be doing his job. These customers buy between $100,000 and several million dollars each year and, if we are entertaining them, our competitors can't, they reason. Experience and success says they are right.

Use your *common sense* and make sure it will really benefit your overall sales goals before you commit your time and money to entertainment as a necessary sales tool, unless it is a company policy.

5. How to Run a Sales Territory

You will need to *prospect every day* with sales presentations to pre-planned prospects. Customer calls as necessary, primarily if you expect to write some new business or a big fill-in. "Fill-ins" are not due to any sales ability, but some customers need *"guidance"* in putting an order together. Some would run out of your brand, if this fits your product line, and would just sell off of the remaining competitive brands in stock. In these cases, you must time your calls and write the "fill-in" order, big enough that your customer has enough stock until the next scheduled "sales call." Try to *sell a "new item"* on every call. You know you made the correct decision when you can say, *"I created a big order and sold a new item today, which would not have been created if I hadn't made the call."*

How many customers are too many to keep? We salesmen, of course, want to keep them all. Time considerations and continuous prospect calls resulting in more and more customers, most that require some service; force a salesman to make hard choices. Like the monkey that can't get his hand out of the jar full of candy because he is greedy and wants it all, *a salesman has to make choices of the most profitable way to spend his time.*

I like to make the following *analogy* to running a successful territory. If you start with 100 spinning pennies representing your customers, you have to keep them spinning or you will lose your customers as they fall and stop spinning. You also have several spinning nickels that represent bigger customers. You have to keep these spinning. You have three spinning quarters. These are very important customers, which must be kept spinning. You have only one *"Silver Dollar"* customer that you can't afford to lose. How should you spend your time and, in addition, prospect for new customers and achieve a sales increase?

Morgan Silver Dollar

First, do some homework. Add all the business the pennies generated last year, whether or not it was your territory at the time. Now total the business produced by the nickels, then quarters and finally the silver dollar. *Prioritize your time accordingly.* You will discover that too much of your time was being spent chasing a disproportionate amount of sales dollars. In other words, *you are spending too much of your sales time spinning pennies* to keep them from falling. If you have any chance for success or to reach the No. 1 spot and the pot of gold, you will have to spend less time keeping the pennies spinning and *most of your time prospecting for more nickel, dime, quarter and silver dollar customers.* Also, sell more to your nickel, dime, quarter and *silver dollar* customers, as they are big enough, if you are good enough, to buy more from you than from your competitors. The pennies, altogether, represent substantial dollars, so ask them to please call the customer service department to place their orders, and call you if they have a question or problem with service. They can receive faster service this way, as you are not always in your office, when traveling. Some pennies will fall and most will keep spinning by themselves. You will spend more and more of your time, as you should spinning bigger and bigger silver coins to get to the top *No. 1 sales and commissions position in your corporation.*

9

You're Burning Daylight

1. The Early Bird Will Win The Gold!

How can you win it all? Start early! How can you open more new accounts and earn more *gold* than everybody else? Start early! How early is early? First sales call at 7:00 am. Night-shift foreman can be called on earlier than that. They work 11:00 pm to 7:00 am so you can see them at 5:00 or 6:00 am, or in the evening after 11:00 pm.

Most salesmen make their first calls between 8:00 and 9:00 am. A salesman who starts his first call at 7:00 am can get one or two sales calls in. Two sales calls times five days equals ten extra calls per week. Two extra calls per work day times 20 days equals 40 extra calls per month times 12 months equals 480 *extra* sales calls by making your first call every day at 7:00 am.

When you are scheduling appointments, make your first call every day at 7:00 am. You will get used to it and have a one hour or more head start on 8:00 and 9:00 am coffee break salesman. Don't lose your advantage on the other end. Stay out there at least until 4:00 pm. You will get "points" from your prospects and customers for being the only salesman still selling at 4:00 pm. "Slave driver" I'm not, but *I know how to win and earn the big money.*

2. Let Your Competitors Watch TV!

We all watch TV and some of us watch TV more than others. Some spend too much of their planning time watching TV and after a hard day's work, we all like to relax and watch our favorite programs. Most of your competitors in your own company and other companies feel the same way. If you have the desire to be No. 1 in your company and in your territory, you will be very selective of the TV time you trade for planning time, report time and thinking how you can do a better, more efficient job than everybody else. If you reserve just one hour each working day, while your day's business is still fresh in your mind and before the special TV programs you like come on, you will enjoy the benefits of five hours more planning than your competitors. At the end of the year, your competitors will wield the "clicker" like Quick Draw McGraw, but you will be No. 1 in sales and income. Steal a few hours every weekend from the family and the TV, as necessary, to plan for optimum results next week. Optimum results, equal *optimum commissions and bonuses.*

3. The Mathematics of Finding Gold

There are approximately 241 net selling days in the year. There are 52 Saturdays and 52 Sundays in a year. There are 7 holidays, 10 days vacation, and 3 days lost to miscellaneous events. Total miscellaneous selling days lost is 20 days per year, give or take a day or two. This totals 124 days lost to weekends, holidays, vacation and sick days or other reasons.

Over one-third of the year is non-productive toward your goal of earning the No. 1 sales honors and monetary rewards in your corporation. This means that over 33 percent of the year, you can't sell anything to your prospects or your customers. How, then, can you sell more than your fellow salesmen in your corporation and your competitors in your industry?

Cheat! On the average, most salesmen will not efficiently utilize the 241 selling days when their prospects and customers are open for business. If you do, you are already way ahead. Here is how to do it.

Saturdays and Sundays account for 104 days of the 124 days "lost" to actual face-to-face selling. Get in the habit of making a regular time every weekend for *success planning and prioritizing the next week's activities.* Steal some weekend time every week to make the next week easier and much more efficient and productive. Most of your competitors won't do this consistently or not at all. However, some will. You are now ahead of most of your competitors. This may seem hard to do. Remember, selling yourself to No. 1 isn't easy. Do your organization and planning during the off hours when your customers are closed to achieve optimum sales results and efficiency when they are open to do business. *Organization, planning, hard work and sacrifice in the off-hours will win out at the end of the year.* Just two hours per weekend will add up to 100 more planning hours than most of your competitors. These 100 or more weekend hours of investment in your success and future will enable you to more completely utilize all 241 selling days when your customers and prospects are *"open for business."* Hard work and dedication will win out over the "silver tongued orator" every time. You are now ahead of 95 percent of all your competitors. Now we'll go after the professional 5 percent.

You will need to spend more time than they do thinking and planning and further organizing your sales strategy:

1. Steal another hour from your weekends or 50 hours more than the other 5 percent will sacrifice.

2. Plan to be off your territory only *one week* instead of two for your family vacation. This gives you 5 days plus 3 hours' jump on your strongest competition. Most of us can only afford one week's vacation anyway, from a time and money standpoint. Your family will understand if you sell it the right way. It will favorably affect the whole family's future to be the No. 1 in sales, commissions and bonuses in the entire corporation, versus just being above the average. Second place doesn't earn a seat for you at the President's table or a promotion; No. 1 does.

3. Plan your vacation during the least busy time in your industry so you are not gone when *"the salmon are running."* Clean up any loose ends before you go and let your customers know whom to call to place an order while you are gone.

4. Work smarter. Improve your product knowledge. Read all your own sales literature. Ask your sales manager for a list of other big customers who buy and are happy with your product or products. How are they using our products? How do they buy? In what quantities do they buy? Is there special pricing? Why? Ask about competition. Why is our product and service a better value than our arch-competitor? If you know more, you will sell more.

5. The top 5 percent are hogging the sales manager's time. You make sure that you hog it more than they do. Your sales management is in sales management because they know how to be successful selling your products. Ask for their help to land the big ones. You set it up and together you will get the job done. Or, would you rather have your sales manager help sell the big one for someone else and vault him to No. 1? You *hog his time selfishly* to gain another big advantage. Make sure you *set up something big* and worthy of his and the company's time, or he will be less eager to answer your call next time. Like you, he also has to increase sales, and will go where and with

whom the big sales increase potential is feasible. *Make him work for you!* Become a team. Make him a hero, but you will be No. 1.

10

Work Ethic and Determination Pay Off Big

1. Work Ethic

The harder you work, the less you worry. The harder you work, the more confident you become. The harder you work, the more successful you are and the more money you earn. The harder you work, the *"luckier"* you get.

Courtesy of George Doyle, Stockbyte Platinum, Getty Images

January 2

Think of January 2 as the start of a long race. The entire sales force of your company starts with a clean sales slate. Your competitors in your territory are at the starting line too. You are all at zero sales. Don't panic, if you have a good *work ethic*, you will come out in the long run at the end of the year in the top 10 percent, or maybe your *burning desire* pushed you to the top 5 percent or even *No. 1 in the company!*

I'm guessing, but I am not far off, that 100 percent of your sales force will want to do well, sell more than last year and earn more money. Some will even want to make the top 10 in sales this year. Most are determined to work hard and achieve their goal. It is important to start fast and strong. Some salesmen will be disorganized. Some, who started slow, will be discouraged when the January sales figures are announced and they are showing a loss as compared with last year. Now they have to sell more to make up the loss and beat last year's February sales and so on. As the year progresses, those with the good work ethic keep going. A race is won at the finish line. Never give up. Consistent hard work will win in the end.

A good number of sales reps with inconsistent flashes of hard work are starting to fall behind and lose some of their will to work harder to catch up. Distractions are abundant if you give in to them. They only put you farther behind the reps that have organized their selling time, which doesn't allow for any distractions. When a salesman agrees to be distracted from his goal, it forces the rep to stop racing while the other reps and his competitors keep running. The distracted rep drops farther behind every time he lets himself be distracted. A distraction is dropping off and picking the kids up after school, taking or picking up a child at ballet lessons and a thousand other important things we would like to do in a perfect world. Every hour a salesman steals from his selling time while all his competitors are selling puts him further behind. Your family must, if you and your family are to be successful, respect your selling time. The alternative is to be always starting a new sales job with no better prognosis for success.

Use all the selling hours every day, without fail, and you will succeed. You have to put in the time, if you plan to succeed. *"You've got to hit the daily!"*

2. Determination

When you know you have the best product, service and company, never give up. A "no" means you haven't presented your product, service and company in such a convincing way that the person would be absolutely nuts to say no. Either that or you have been talking to an uninterested party. You have the wrong person! In most cases, the "buyer" is the wrong person to which to make your sales presentation. He is not expected to know the inner workings of every department. He is only interested in price. As you are not selling price and have a high quality product, your price will be too high for him to consider.

Don't let a receptionist tell you who to see or that you want the buyer! Call into the company you want to sell and which uses your category of products. Your present customers can provide the titles of company personnel who understand, use and like your products. Connect with those same job titles in the prospect company and arrange to make a presentation. He will understand the benefits of your product over the product he is using now. He will recognize the increased productivity, safety and cost savings, even at your quality pricing. The production manager, engineer and plant manager will see the savings and lack of problems by using a superior product. They will *"tell"* the buyer to place an order immediately at this price, period. Now, the buyer can't say "no!"

If you don't succeed with the first presentation, keep trying at reasonable intervals to present a different product or some other customer's success with the original product you presented. It's not a good practice to just stop by to say hello. They are too busy to chat and if you don't have anything important to tell them about how they might improve their business, it is better if you don't stop and hurt yourself by not being granted future appointments.

Determination will take us to places where others will not go or spend the long-term time sometimes required. I spent *seven years* working to secure the testing and then approval of a water-based degreaser to replace a solvent that had been banned from use by EPA on a future date. I started working to get testing and approvals for a water-based degreaser replacement at the major aerospace giants in Southern California several years before the Vapor Degreaser Solvent would be banned. My water-based degreaser was finally approved, after years of testing, as "sole-source" by Northrop Grumman in the Los Angeles area for use in several degreasing tanks into which Boeing 747 body panels were cleaned and rinsed as the first step in their final processing before assembly at Boeing in the Seattle area.

At the same time I had been working with three different engineers and the lead chemist at McDonnell Douglas, now Boeing, in Long Beach. It was the engineer's responsibility to choose a water-based degreaser that would clean the manufacturing oils, grease and finger prints from the parts, but to be safe to work on aluminum and the workers. Most water-based cleaners are highly alkaline, which will etch (eat) the aluminum. The problem was to find a water-based cleaner that will clean the soils without etching the aluminum. Boeing, because of the now imminent ban on the Vapor Degreaser solvent, built a 50,000 gallon aqueous degreaser tank and a sister tank for a RO (Reverse Osmosis) water rinse tank. All the chemical salesmen were drooling over this "state of the art" 50,000 gallon tank, which at ten parts (water) to one part (degreaser) meant a 5,000 gallon sale, (equivalent to ninety-one drums) just to charge the tank. Replenishment water-based degreaser will be added on a regular basis to keep the concentration and pH at the same level as the original charge. My *determination and persistence* paid off, not to mention my company's *chemists* for formulating the perfect product for this special and unusual situation. Our product safety was critical as it was used to clean major aluminum airliner and Delta II rocket sections.

Five thousand gallons of The Brulin Company's "Formula 815GD" was ordered to charge the Boeing Company's 50,000 gallon tank. The norm was to sell 55 gallon drums of the various chemicals, but this order called for a *tank truck.* I was waiting for the tanker when it arrived early in the morning at Boeing in Long Beach, California. Why was I there? *Service!* I had to make sure the tank truck driver kept the nozzle of the hose from the tank truck *under the water* as he was unloading the cleaner/degreaser into the tank of "RO" water or too much foam might be created, which would not be good!

Bob Felgen, in suit behind tank truck, delivering 5,000 gallons of water-based Degreaser to Boeing in Long Beach, California

A footnote: Attention to every detail is important in selling. I didn't want a great sale to a huge and important customer like Boeing to be delivered by the average dirty tank truck with tar, oil and dirt on the tank and one delivery short of the junk yard. My company hired the tank line and we were their customer so I called the trucking company a told them this shipment was going to our most important customer and I wanted our product to arrive in a *new tank truck*. The material inside the tank truck must be "squeaky clean" and free of any and all contamination from previous shipments. An old, dirty tanker would give the perception we were sloppy and that would make the cargo "suspect". I told the manager this would be a photo opportunity for his company as pictures would be taken and copies sent to them. We got a brand new tank truck.

3. Always Tell the Truth

Always tell the truth to your customers and your company. If you do your job, there should be absolutely no reason to tell a lie. None of us have a good enough memory to remember exactly what we told each customer about our products or ourselves. If a salesman stretches the truth all over his territory, he will *always* get caught. When you always tell the truth, you have nothing to worry about. You don't have to try to remember what story you told someone, because everyone was told the same story, *the truth*.

4. Expense Reports

Never "steal" from the hand that feeds you, your company. It reflects badly on your honesty and character. I am talking about *"padding"* the expense account. There are many justifications that can be rationalized, but it comes out as *dishonesty* to every one else. If you are a professional salesman, you are smart enough to know you earn the big dollars by spending your time planning and selling and not to ever jeopardize your job and reputation and take time to steal a few bucks. *Besides, your sales management knows what you are doing,* as they have been and are on the road, too, and they know what is realistic and what is not. The cheating salesman will eventually get caught and be very embarrassed and ashamed, *which destroys self-esteem and all his confidence* and effectiveness, if he still has his job.

One good salesman I knew put down a person on his expense report as a lunch guest for a certain date and amount. In the meantime, back at the home office they had previously received notice of the death of this same lunch guest and customer before this salesman's bogus luncheon date. It was obvious the salesman had not made the call or he would have known *the woman he "took to lunch" died the week before.* He never lived that down.

5. The Joke Is On You

The decision maker at a big corporation doesn't have time during business hours for salesmen who waste time by telling jokes to "break the ice." A salesman isn't selling jokes nor is the decision maker interested in buying "jokes." Leave the jokes to the professional comedians. A professional salesman should use this precious and critical time to suggest "ideas" on how best to utilize his product to benefit the decision maker and his corporation.

Also, some jokes are in poor taste and could offend the business contact the salesman is trying to impress. The joke-telling salesmen feel they have an obligation to pollinate their territory with a new joke each go-around. These *"sample case comedians"* are oblivious to the fact that every joke is not appreciated by everyone, if not anyone. Salesmen should be businessmen, who are professional in their approach, *offering ideas that benefit the decision maker and his corporation.*

So many jokes are at the expense of someone, religious or ethnic groups, sexual and many other offensive or questionable subjects to a lot of people. As we sell to people, it is wise to stick to the business reason you are there, to sell something. No joke!

6. I Have Miles and Miles to Go and Promises to Keep

Or should it be "promises to forget?" This is one of the biggest traps that salesmen walk right into is to open our big mouths and promise the prospect or customer that you will do something nice for him. The prospect thinks you are going to be a very good salesman, but later finds out the promised deed never happened and the "good salesman" thoughts are gone. It would have been better not to promise anything, if you are not going to follow through with your promise. Apologies don't get you back to where you were and now you're on the defensive. Not a good way to sell.

Be very stingy with your promises. It will hurt you if your promises aren't kept. *If you must make a promise to do something, do it right away.* After the "promise call," when you get to your car, use your cell phone and call headquarters and order the item or literature that you promised. Then post on your account page that the item was ordered and the date. On your next callback, they will have received the item you promised, and you are now in a good position to get an order. Look at the account sheet before the return call, as it will remind you that you had ordered something for them and can ask if they have received the item. The customer will be impressed that you remembered. You didn't, but you looked at your notes on your customer sheet. Salesmen are always in a hurry to get to the next sales situation, but if you drive away without completing this call first, after several more calls you will forget what you promised and now it's too late to call the office. So, tomorrow you want to get started selling and more unfulfilled promises are made and so on. *Salesmen in general are notorious for making promises they don't keep.*

Dilbert ©: Scott Adams/Dist. by United Feature Syndicate, Inc.

11

Think Gold

Image courtesy of www.sidereus.org/MONEY
The Sidereus Foundation is a member of the Starfields Network
www.Starfields.net

1. Ideas

Salesmen not only sell products, they *sell IDEAS!* If a salesman is trying to sell a product but the decision maker has some of this same type products that are not "moving." *give him an "idea"* how to sell your product and also get rid of his dead stock and he will now be interested and buy your product. The salesman can go two ways.

One way is to say he is sorry that the widgets he has in stock aren't selling but ours have been selling well at the biggest store in town. This guy is not going to buy more widgets until he sells what he has.

The other way is the salesman can suggest running a co-op ad in the local newspaper on your newer widgets and the rep hands him the "ad mat." Suggest either he return the competitor's widgets or get their vendor to either split a sale ad, discounting the old widgets to get rid of them or donate them to a charity. At least with an *"idea,"* the salesman can turn a negative around. The salesman must pre-think many *ideas* for different situations he has run into before. He has to have "ad mats" to cover his various products and his company's OK to pay 50 percent of these local ads. Usually there is a minimum order required to earn the co-op advertising. *Sell the publicity for his store* and *the sales and profit the ad will generate. Paint a benefits picture.* The first salesman was fishing with an empty hook. The second salesman at least put a big juicy worm on his hook. Who is most likely to *"strike" gold?*

2. Ingenuity

Ingenuity is "the quality of being cleverly inventive or resourceful." This separates the professional salesman from the many ordinary salesmen. Here is one example.

By altering the corporate order pad in the field, a salesman was able to get approval for much bigger orders from the ultra-conservative intimate apparel buyers in mid-western small to medium size department stores. Any salesman would be lucky to get out of a store with a few hundred dollars sale. A woman's brassiere is packaged two or three to a box in each size. The corporate order pad used one line for each cup size—A, B, C and D—or four lines of the order pad. If a buyer bought five new styles for the new season, it took 20 lines. If the buyer added sizes "AA" and "DD," times five styles, it takes ten more lines. Now the order takes 30 lines—one full page and part of the second page.

When the buyer sees one full page or two pages, her perception is the order is too big and has to be cut. The buyer will usually want to cut some end-sizes or one of the new styles or, in the buyer's mind, will be way over the season's "open-to-buy" limit. The order, as written in the corporate format, was perceived to be too big by the number of lines and pages.

With a simple field change in the way some unnamed corporate person designed the order form, *the professional salesman was able to get the same order approved without changes because the perception of the order being too big had been eliminated.*

How did he do it? Instead of using up a full line for "A" and a full line for "B" and so on, he wrote A, B, C and D across the top of the order form. Under each letter there are three, four or five sizes. Instead of using four, five or six lines for one style, this *salesman's ingenuity enabled him to cram the same dollars, and all of the original order, on only five lines instead of 30.* The buyer's perception when signing the order was that it was small and well within the budget. This was accomplished all across the territory and *resulted in an increase in sales of over 600 percent.*

When the truck full of brassiere boxes arrived at the loading dock, the buyer must have been shocked, and when the bill came, it used most of the season's intimate apparel budget. The buyer was still within the total budget, but there was very little left for the other brands. You might think these buyers will now cut you off the next time. Not only did they not complain because they had the best sales increase ever, for the first time didn't run out of sizes for their customers. How could they think of dropping the line now, when all those customers will be back with repeat demand for your brand?

By the way, the corporation didn't alter their order form, but did not complain either.

Always keep thinking of how you can gain an advantage over your competitors. No lower price, no business lunch, no big smile and no hot deal, *just use a little ingenuity and common sense.*

3. Sell Yourself First

If they don't like you, they are less likely to buy from you. Dress appropriately, smile, be pleasant and don't argue. Be agreeable and, if they are rude and nasty, don't get mad and "burn your bridges behind you" or you will run out of prospects. If you react positively to a negative situation, you might save the day and turn the situation around. *Always stay positive.* In my experience, some of the toughest, most negative prospects became my best and most friendly customers. You have to be like a *"wolf in sheep's clothing."*

Also, *be like a chameleon* that changes colors according to his environment. In other words, agree with the prospect that you are trying to convince to go with you, your company and products, no matter what political party, religion or anger about his boss he is expounding to you. Just listen and allow him to let off steam and when he calms down, *ask for the order.* By listening and nodding apparent approval, he will think you agree with him and automatically like you and be more apt to deal with you and give his new friend an order. If, on the other hand, you bring your soap-box and tell him what you think to defend your favorite cause, which is the opposite of his outspoken views, you have lost this prospect forever. *You may win this battle, but you have just lost the war.*

You have to keep hanging in there, no matter what, if you really want to sell the account. You have to want to sell them more than they don't want you to sell them! Brush aside the negatives and go right on with the positives. Anyone can "sell" someone who will buy everything from anyone that walks in the door because they probably don't have any intention of paying for it. The professional salesman will go after the big, tough ones, persevere, keep their professional composure, win the prospects over and eventually earn the first order and a long time customer and friend. Lose your temper or pout, none of this will ever happen.

Also, *sell yourself to your sales manager.* Get him thinking positively about you and your sales ability. *Keep in close touch.* Let him know what you are doing. When your sales manager travels with you**,** *have everything well planned, be organized and have appointments with big prospects and customers.* If appropriate, set up a lunch or dinner with a big prospect or your biggest customer, but before you do this, check with your sales manager. Think of, and treat, your sales manager as a friend who is helping you get more business and earn more money. If you are working hard but not doing as well as you should, your sales manager is giving his time and experience to help you. Ask him how you can do better. *Stay positive and enthusiastic and be eager to learn.* Help him give a positive report to his superiors. If the negative talk starts flowing, it's only a matter of time. *Keep it positive!* If you are working hard, and have a positive attitude and excellent product knowledge, you have absolutely nothing to be ashamed about. Hold your head up high and keep going and you will make it, *with your sales manager on your side.*

4. Servicing Customers

Look at your customers as your "bread and butter" accounts. They provide you with a base of income freeing up time for your major effort, *prospecting. New business, new customers, give you 100 percent sales and commission increases.* If you write a "fill-in" order, it is probably about the same as last year and there is no increase. The name of the game and the big money is realized with *sales increase.* If you spend most of your time with your customers writing fill-in orders and think you're a good salesman because you wrote an order, think again. It doesn't take "salesmanship," or a college education, to go into a friendly customer, take a stock count and fill-in with items that are missing. Selling a new item to a repeat customer will give you an increase with that account and it is worthwhile, but not the 100 percent increase generated if the same item were sold to a new customer.

On the other side of the coin, you can't afford to neglect your customers altogether. Your large customers will require service on a regular call schedule. They may require technical assistance from your company and you will have to be there to make sure the problem is handled to the complete satisfaction of your customer. Don't let the tech rep handle the problem alone and let your customer feel that you don't care.

Also, if the tech rep can't handle the problem properly or completely, your customer may be forced to call your competitor. No late apology will now get this customer back. If you were there, as you should have been, you would have made sure someone in your company corrected the problem. They would be much less likely to call a competitor if their salesman was working to help them.

In planning your time, put yourself in your customer's place. What service and attention would you need or reasonably expect from your vendor and your sales representative? Smaller customers won't expect their sales rep to call on them often. They are used to calling their reorders in to the company. Very few competitive sales reps call on them and they are usually loyal. Call on your most important customers on a regular schedule and try and sell them something new while you're there. If an *emergency occurs at a major customer* and they call for you to come in and help them, *drop everything* and get there as fast as you can. Your scheduled plan is very important to your success, but common sense and self-interest tell you to hell with the schedule, *saving the major "Silver Dollar" account is more important than anything else.* I'm not making this up. This actually happened to a very good salesman who was extremely organized and detail oriented. One day he got an urgent call from one of his very biggest multi-branch department store customers who asked him to come into headquarters right away to straighten out a problem. The salesman called the customer back and told them he could come *next Tuesday.* These are people that aren't used to being told "no!" *This major account was gone,* and so were all the commissions. When in doubt, always use common sense.

5. Confidentiality

For a salesman's own good and future success, he should treat each customer as if it was his own family that doesn't want their business broadcast all over town. Corporations, even to a much greater extent, do not want their business operations discussed with anyone, and especially with competitors. When a sales rep tells in detail how his product is utilized at a competitor, he is also telling this customer he will tell all about their operation to his competitors or anyone else to help make a sale. The company he is telling will now clam-up or buy from someone else. *Military contractors are especially sensitive.* It is best to adopt the golden rule of Las Vegas, *"Everything that happens here, stays here!"*

12

A Secretary That Sits On Your Lap

1. The Lap Top Computer

Many corporations give their salesmen laptop computers to use. It is a faster way to exchange information and it's in writing, for the record. The days of the pager and sending information by fax machine are declining. Cell phones are a huge help to outside salesmen. The two problems are no one is personally answering their phone anymore and the danger of placing calls while driving, plus the missed possible visual prospects. All in all, the cell phone comes in handy for a salesman if used wisely and safely. Corporations and a good number of customers now prefer requests and information via e-mail rather than by telephone.

Most professional salesmen today are proficient in using computers and own their own desk-top or laptop computers. If a corporation does not furnish a laptop and portable printer, the professional salesman should buy his own and it will be tax-deductible as a non-reimbursed business expense.

Professional outside salesmen always take their laptop computer with them while on the road and e-mail their reports and technical questions to the home office from their motel or hotel room. They can pull up information such as "material safety data sheets" and print them for the next day's appointments. Customer sales information can be pulled up and used to prepare the next day's sales calls.

Weekly expenses submitted by e-mail can now be turned around in two or three days and the money wired into your bank account, all while you are on the road. In the past, expenses submitted to the sales manager for approval by mail had to wait in his in-box until he got back from a trip and wait until he had time to sign it and send it to Accounting. Accounting would cut a check and mail it to you. In the meantime, you were out on the road again spending more of your own money. Total reimbursement time used to take two to three weeks. Then you would have to take it to the bank and make the deposit. This, alone, makes the computer worthwhile.

The salesman can review e-mail messages and make his replies from a motel in a timely manner and lessen this work on the weekend. If a technical question is asked while working with a customer and the person you need to ask is on the road, he can be reached through e-mail that evening and the answer could be received the same evening or by next morning before leaving your room. E-mail is an excellent way to communicate between salesmen and their sales managers, or other salesmen if a need arises. Formal personalized quotations can be printed on the corporate letterhead in the field and then offered in a professional sales presentation the next day. Small portable printers are usually furnished with the lap-tops. These printers are easily packed in a suitcase.

Computers help a salesman be better organized and a better in-house communicator and help his presentations and quotations look more professional. *But, a computer never sold anything!* Remember that. A computer can be insidious in stealing selling time in the name of, and in place of, face-to-face selling. The computer is merely supportive to the salesman. Don't let it use up any of the prime face-to-face selling time in each sales day when prospects are available and waiting to be sold.

2. The World Is On Your Belt

The cell phone gives the professional salesman a world-wide stage. A salesman can call and sell anywhere in the world, anyone you want to, unless you have a defined territory. Even then, you must think big and utilize this salesman's tool to great advantage as the cell phone gives you the opportunity to make many more sales contacts in a day. Program your prospects and customer's names and phone numbers into your cell phone for speed and safety. A salesman can get answers *now* from the home office, call ahead to prospects and customers ask customers for their reorder or ask them to buy a special promotion. It enables a salesman to get around his or her territory faster with short supply promotions and insure early delivery.

In the days I covered five states, I used to send post cards ahead of a planned two week trip around the territory announcing I was coming to call on them to show the "new line." Every phone call was a long distance charge in those days. Also, while in the car, no one could reach me. Now, all nation-wide long distance cell phone calls are "free" within the minutes of your service provider's plans from which a salesman chooses.

Another vital benefit the cell phone provides is a salesman's *safety*. Today, if a salesman has car trouble or has an accident, he can call for help immediately. I was riding with the Little Rock salesman at night driving to make a presentation the next morning to Wal-Mart in Bentonville, Arkansas when the salesman's car ran out of gas! It was pitch-dark and the two lane road was lined with trees and it was desolate!

I had remembered seeing the movie "Deliverance" with Burt Reynolds and John Voight, where some "city boys" ran into some unfriendly locals in the woods and it was nasty. There we were, two "city boys," and it was "Deliverance" all over again! We were "apprehensive to say the least! The closest thing to a cell phone in those days was Dick Tracy's "wrist radio", which we didn't have either. I won't finish the rest of the story except to tell you that after a long wait a man in an old pick-up truck, with a rifle attached to a rack on the back window, stopped and took the frightened salesman with him and told me I should stay with the car! Now I was alone and was plain scared! I was also worried about the young salesman. I guess it turned out OK as I am writing this, but a word to the wise: Always fill your gas tank when you plan to work with your sales manager, especially in "Deliverance" country.

Selling is communication! The cell phone, besides *safety*, offers a great selling advantage to the professional salesmen who integrate it into their selling strategy. Use the cell phone fully and *safely* to achieve your goals and communicate yourself to the top of the pack and the gold.

3. The BlackBerry

The BlackBerry is a wireless handheld device which supports "push" e-mail, mobile telephone, text messaging, internet faxing, Web-browsing and other wireless information. It was developed by Research In Motion (RIM) and delivers information over the wireless data networks of cellular telephone companies.

BlackBerry is primarily known for its ability to send and receive e-mail anywhere it has access. The BlackBerry is more convenient to use during the day while on the road than a laptop computer.

There are now a number of third party commercial applications available for BlackBerry. One application is for sales force automation.

The ability to read e-mail that is received in real time, anywhere, has made BlackBerry quite addictive and it has earned the nickname "CrackBerry."

The latest BlackBerry models, the 8700 series, offers "Push" mail, Web browsing, and other mobile data applications, together with premium mobile phone with dedicated phone keys, smart dialing, conference calling, speed dialing, call forwarding, speaker phone hands-free use and Bluetooth® support for use with headsets and car kits.

4. Bluetooth®

Bluetooth enables salesmen to make and receive phone calls via their cell phones, but through in-car systems. They can be factory installed or aftermarket installed. Both your cell phone and car must be Bluetooth-compatible.

Salesmen can operate their cell phones either through their car's controls or via hands-free voice activation. Many automotive brands offer Bluetooth-compatible vehicles as standard equipment.

Bluetooth also enables short-range wireless connections between desktop and notebook computers, handhelds, personal digital assistants, mobile phones, camera phones, printers, digital cameras, headsets, keyboards and a computer mouse.

For a salesman, Bluetooth offers a safe way to contact prospects and customers during the many selling hours spent in his or her car. Also a salesman can be contacted by a customer, home office or his wife in an emergency, while driving safely, hands-free.

5. Information Technology Today: "Smartphones" or "Pocket PC's"

All major wireless cell phone companies offer "Smartphones" or "Pocket PC's" that use Windows Mobile 5.0 software such as "Microsoft Office Word Mobile, Microsoft Excel Mobile and Microsoft Office PowerPoint Mobile." A salesman or sales manager today, with the proper equipment, can access and send e-mail messages, and pull-up sales and customer information as well as wireless communication while on the road making sales presentations.

Microsoft Windows Mobile enabled devices help salesmen and sales managers access the business information they need while on the road and where the use of their lap-top is not feasible.

A salesman needs current information on the customers and prospects he or she is trying to sell. Whether it comes from posting information to an account sheet or getting information electronically, a salesman must have current information to be effective over and way beyond his or her competitors.

Real time information is the ammunition that enables generals and salesmen to win their battles. Information creates opportunities. Real time, up-to-date information equals sales. Information is the fuel that propels you to the top!

On November 3, 2006 Google, the web search leader, introduced a custom version of its Gmail service that can run on any phone with Java software. Google says it is an application and doesn't run through a browser so it looks and feels like Gmail on the desktop.

Keep an eye on Motorola. In September of '06, Motorola paid $3.9-billion to purchase "Symbol Technologies, Inc., maker of portable bar code scanners and customized hand-held computers.

On November 11, 2006 Motorola announced it was buying Good Technology, Inc. a Santa Clara, California firm that provides computing software and services for competing "smartphone" companies. Good Technology, Inc. will join Motorola's "Mobile Devices" unit which has prospered due to the runaway success of its "RAZR" phones. This should raise the prospects for its new Motorola Q™ device as consumer demand for e-mail phones explodes.

This is the latest technology at this time to get information in real time and there will be better and smaller business communication devices and software in the future. Do your homework and keep up with the latest technology available to enable you to know more, faster than your competitors at any given time and close more sales. Also check out the Apple "smartphone" called "iPhone," available in June 2007 at $499 through Cingular Wireless.

Information you need when you need it!

13

Seek and You Shall Find

1. Prospecting For Gold

Ask your customers who their competitors are. Buy the Industrial Directory from the Chamber of Commerce in each of your cities. Buy the telephone books for your major cities and look up your industry in phone books in the small town as you pass through. Some of the largest prospects are located in small towns for the lower labor costs. Big city newspapers will have marketing information books that give complete information on the companies in their market. Look up industries and companies in the Thomas Guide at your library. Every industry has an Association. Call them and ask for an industry directory. There may be a charge, unless you are or become a member. Read the business section of your major newspaper every day. As you drive through your territory and see a potential customer, make a note of it on a recorder and look them up on the internet later. If you have the time, stop now and check it out, otherwise it may be several weeks or months before you get back to them. Use your computer to find information about major companies you know of before you make your initial presentation. Post the appropriate information on your account or prospect sheet. Use a separate sheet for other important information not vital to have on your account sheet, but important as a refresher to your initial presentation.

After your presentation, place this extra sheet in your account or prospect's file. Each customer and prospect should have a manila file folder. You can create a customer or prospect sheet on your laptop, but you will have to carry it with you all the time. Good, consistent record-keeping is something most salesmen don't like to take the time to do. Salesmen aren't accountants. Salesmen like to move fast and rely on their great personality. Personality does not cause a prospect to part with his money. *Facts and information that benefit the prospect or customer over and above what he is using now, are the keys* in earning an order or a new customer. This information comes from your records. Record keeping is not being an accountant. It is being smart and giving your self every advantage in coming up with an informed, well thought out sales presentation that considers all the *advantages to the prospect* or customer. Your sales presentation is a test of your knowledge about the prospect's business, and *how your product will be beneficial to his business.* Think of your account record about your prospect as a *"crib sheet."* Most, if not all, professional sales representatives rely on their records to become successful sales professionals. Which would you rather buy from—Mr. Personality with his wild claims and no substance, or from someone who did his homework and *fits his product to your needs?*

2. More on Prospecting

No matter how good you are, every sales territory can expect to lose some customers. As good as you are there are also good sales reps working for your competitors that may have something new that may be perceived to be better than what they are buying from you. Most customers are loyal if you have given them good attention and service. If there is a big advantage to them to make a change, they almost have to in order to keep their job.

Some smaller companies go out of business. You may lose some customers to a price increase by your company. Any price increase induces some to start looking to see if there is a better deal out there. It's your job to *sell the price increase* so this won't happen. Some customers are lost as a result of a personnel change, where the new person likes another company or sales rep he has worked with in the past. A salesman can lose a customer when the founder of that customer dies, and his heirs sell the company or change suppliers.

Some situations, over which you have no control, such as the person in charge of buying your products is obvious about wanting something "under the table." In most cases, your or their company policy forbids giving or receiving gifts, but if not, it's a lose, lose, situation, because no matter what you would give to get the business, there is always someone who will give a bigger or better gift. Eventually, this person is caught and fired. You don't want yourself or your company involved or banned. There is no future in these kinds of sales. There should be a "red light" over this kind of buyer's doors! This should not be confused with giving a small *"thank you"* gift at Christmas *as a token of your appreciation.* Some might say, what's the difference? The difference is giving to get the business as opposed to giving a small token of appreciation for the business and working relationship you have enjoyed all year. It's a difference that possibly only a professional salesman can recognize. *To the professional, it's the difference between a "red light" salesman and a saint.*

I feel I must make a proviso to the above as I never knew a "Master Salesman" who could be considered a "Saint!" In some situations a colorblind "street smart" salesman can see the red light as *green*. An opportunity to "trade" small dollars invested for big dollar commission returns. Professional salesmen have to make many decisions based on their experience, whether a given situation is worth the time and expense or is it a "Black Hole" situation?

The above loss of customers, hopefully not your fault, but loss anyway, is known as "attrition." This is why you must continually prospect and sell new customers. You must replace your territory's lost customers to keep your current sales volume and commissions. You also must add enough new business by prospecting to earn the expected sales increase. Then you must close more prospects yet to have any chance to be No. 1 in sales with your company. You have to prospect every day, efficiently in a pre-planned pattern. Looking around for prospects without a plan or an appointment is wasting your valuable time. The clock is ticking. Instead, use your weekend planning time to choose and prioritize your prospect calls. Use your business directories and your knowledge of big businesses in your industry that you are not now selling. In other words prospect where gold can be found. Think big. Think big money. Think gold!

3. A Big Farm System of Prospects Will Harvest the Gold

Where else would Major League teams get good, experienced players? The majors would die out if they didn't have a farm system of *major league prospects.*

It is the same for all salesmen everywhere. A salesman needs a large farm team of *prospects* in the wings at all times if he is to be successful. Some companies have a minimum acceptable number of three new customers every month. In six months you better have sold 18 new accounts and have at least 36 prospects by year-end that you have brought up to the majors! This is just the minimum expected new accounts. To accomplish this and more, each salesman must have a very large "farm team" of prospects to "bring up" to customer status.

A salesman *must* make a lot of prospect sales calls every day. There are so many potential prospects in any territory they couldn't all be covered in a salesman's working lifetime. The bigger the farm team of quality prospects the more chances a salesman will have to far exceed "minimum quota." Picture yourself with several prospects that you have called on, given your sales pitch and left some literature.

You have no farm team. You have not built a farm system of prospects that continuously feed you quality new customers. You need to think big farm team of over 100 prospects. Some will never make the majors. You know who is ready to play and you will tell them of the great value added benefits to them, of coming up to the majors on your team. You will find that with a big farm team of major prospects, you will open far more than the minimum three new customers per month that is required. If you only do what is "required," you will not be in the big money league.

To create a huge farm system for yourself, you must make a large number of prospect presentations *daily*! A salesman needs to get in the habit of always doing this, *forever*. As you "close" prospects and bring them up, you have to replace them in spades to stay even. You will become better with your *presentation* and *close* and you will sell more prospects on the first call. Every salesman needs to know, who are the most likely prospects to bring up to the majors? He must keep very good records on prospect information sheets. Right after every prospect call is the best and only time when you know the most about the prospect. Remember were talking about hundreds of prospect calls. So write down everything that you know about this prospect and what is needed to sell him. Prioritize your callbacks in your own way so you will know when you should make the follow-up call and what points to stress to close the sale. You might mark your record sheet with "hot," "warm," "cold" or "dead." Different color tabs can be used to grade the potential of each prospect, as you will forget after many other calls.

Call back *timing* is of *critical importance*! They will forget you, your company and what you are selling if you let more than two weeks go by. It's very important that you post your prime call back date in your calendar book, or you have wasted your time on the first call. Don't tear their sheet out if you miss the exact two-week date. Call the prospect, remind them of whom you are and that you stopped a few weeks ago and have the information they requested and would like to make an appointment at their convenience. "Would 7:00 am Monday morning be OK?" If a prospect in the salesman's opinion has little potential, list him as such on your prospect sheet and don't put him on your two-week schedule. If you think it's worth a call back in the future, post him for a possible call six months later. You can decide at that time if you want to make another call. That is why it's so important to *write down everything right after every call* so you can make the proper judgment six month's later. Want to open the most new accounts in your company? Build yourself the biggest and best quality "farm team!"

4. Utilize Your Cell Phone to Get Appointments

The person you are trying to talk to is usually on the factory floor or "in a meeting" and you must leave a message on an answering machine or hang up and try again at a different time. If you leave a "blind message" such as, "My name is so and so with the ABC Co. and my number is—. Please return my call". In most cases, they will not return your call. They don't know your name and probably don't know your company and if they do, they will know the company and don't want to bother explaining why they don't want to work with another vendor. They hope by not returning your call you will take the hint and not call back. Discouraging, but don't give up. Your competitors will face the same treatment and most will give up.

You know you have the best product on the market so it must be better than the product this prospect is using. So, try again early in the morning when the person you need to talk with is probably at his desk and you might catch him or her. Remember, you're trying to get an appointment. Don't try and sell your product over the phone. If you still get the machine you can do two things: 1. Tell him, briefly, why you want an appointment with him and leave your number again. Whet his appetite to hear more, but keep it brief. You might write out the best way to get your product or service benefits across to him in the least amount of words. 2. Hang up and try again until you can catch him at his desk. If you keep leaving no meat messages to fill up his machine, he'll never talk to you.

Early in my selling career, I was selling "3-M" copy machines and was getting the same old brush off at the reception window of the "Brotherhood of Teamsters" union headquarters in Chicago. At the time, the president of the union (not Jimmy Hoffa) was in the Chicago Tribune newspaper almost every day. I cut out the favorable articles, copied them in all the colors, sent them in for the president to see and asked for a demonstration. I was ushered into the headquarters, gave my best demonstration and sold the machine on the spot. I gave the union president something that was of interest to him, articles about him and in living color. This is called *determination, ingenuity* and *salesmanship!*

If the person you want to talk to employs a secretary, do not start selling to her. Ask if you can make an appointment at a convenient time for the prospect. They all will then ask you: "What is this in reference to?" Be specific and full of confidence, but not arrogant. She can be a friend. After you have done your brief best to convey the importance of a meeting, she will always say, "Oh, you're a salesman!" Depending on how you present yourself and your case for a meeting, you may or may not be given an appointment this time. If not, try again another time with a better story and bring her candy if she's thin or flowers or perfume if she's heavy. A company pen won't do it.

It is a hard situation to get a meeting over the phone, but after some failures and some successes, you will learn what it takes using your experience, knowledge and personality to devise a technique to get the meetings you must have to be successful. Your *desire* and *determination* will push you to succeed and you will never let yourself become discouraged, and will always keep going toward your goal of being No. 1 in your company and in your territory in sales and *income*. Why go to all that work and trouble? Because being the *"best"* is a wonderful feeling. Being the *"best"* earns you the respect of your peers, the company president and all the executives. Your family will be proud of you; will appreciate the *extra earnings* and *bonus* and very possibly a *promotion*. Your *account base* and *earnings* will be much bigger next year because of all the *new customers* you brought in this year. Keep selling new customers and every year your territory *earnings will grow* and selling ability and confidence will get you through any door. All it takes is *hard work, desire, organization, planning, determination, persistence,* "*salesmanship*" *and your cell phone.*

5. Keep Your Eyes Open For Opportunities

If you are listening to the car radio, your mind is not completely on the business opportunities you are driving by. You are driving past thousands of sales and commission dollars, hell-bent to your next destination. It is the same as driving to get a fill-in order that has the value of lead as you whiz by hundreds of opportunities that have the value of silver and gold.

Here are a couple of examples. While on the way to see a small customer, the salesman was driving past a canoe rental company on the Russian River in Northern California. As he drove past, he noticed the canoes were aluminum. He was part way across the river bridge when he stopped, backed up and turned into the road where the aluminum canoes were being welded and were being readied for the coming canoe season. The canoes were upside down and lined up as far as you could see. There were over one thousand aluminum canoes that were oxidized and had black algae on their bottoms. This was the aluminum brightener salesman's dream. This is called a *"visual,"* a lead you produced with your own eyes. This is an aside, but it is vital if you are to make a sale on the spot, now. When on the road, *always carry your best demo samples* with you as it might be a long time until you pass this way, with eyes wide open, again.

A small amount of a gallon sample of concentrated aluminum brightener was poured on a canoe's black bottom, it sizzled a minute or two while a bucket of water was secured, and when rinsed, was shiny silver. No brushing was required.

Three 55-gallon drums were ordered on the spot plus the equipment to dispense. This was a new customer and this order amount was *100 percent increase dollars.* By paying attention, the salesman sold more with his alertness than he would sell the customer to which he was headed.

The "visual" customers are pure gravy. Your competitors will zoom right by. One more example of how *big* a *"visual"* customer can be. Actually, this salesman cheated and turned on his radio, as it was a route he had driven many times. (That reminds me that a salesman should alternate the areas through which he travels, to discover new prospects.) On the news, he heard that the USS Coral Sea was due to go under the Golden Gate Bridge at 11:00 am that morning, and would dock in Alameda. The salesman's destination was the Oakland Airport where he had several big accounts. The salesman, who had always been interested in aircraft and aircraft carriers, thought how much fun it would be to sell an aircraft carrier and what a hero he would be to his company, not to mention the commission involved. He was already selling approved safe aircraft cleaners next door at the airport. So, why not give it a try?

USS "Coral Sea" sailing under the "Golden Gate" Bridge
Photo courtesy of US Navy

So he did give it a try and drove right into the Alameda Naval Air Station where the aircraft carrier was docked. (This was before September 11, 2001.) He asked for the "Air Department" as he sells aircraft cleaners. They weren't interested in aircraft cleaners, but were looking for a good flight deck and hangar deck cleaner for their two huge automatic riding scrubbers. If the flight deck isn't squeaky clean and an aircraft or other big deck equipment slides off into the ocean in rough seas, the air officer in charge will never be promoted. The flight deck gets greasy from the catapults, landing cables and heavy equipment on the decks.

Here is where *product knowledge* and *demonstration experience* is vital. The flight deck is covered in non-skid material like rough sand paper. This will cause nearly all of the detergent cleaners to generate too much foam. Under conditions at sea, the deck would foam and create bubbles, which is not acceptable. You only have *one shot* at recommending the exact correct cleaner for your big test for all the marbles. Again, you cheat before the big demo. The sales rep asked if he could try the two or three cleaners he thought most likely would do the job they want. He tried a heavy-duty grease cutter he knew would cut the heavy grease and oil on the flight deck. If he had tried this degreaser in the competitive formal demonstration, he would have been thrown off the ship. It emulsified the grease into a milky mixture of grease, degreaser and water and turned the deck white in the trial spot and was extremely difficult to remove from the deck. The salesman tried another non-emulsifying cleaner, but it didn't cut all the grease. Finally, he had brought the logical industrial strength, low-suds cleaner built for use in automatic scrubbers, but to scrub the aisles in department stores. It did a good job on a small test spot on the flight deck with a hand brush so this was his choice for the formal test against competition. He wasn't sure it could cut the heavy grease on the carrier deck, but should work well in their big "Tennant 550" riding scrubber. The Air Department officer liked the spot test results.

Tennant 550 Riding Scrubber
Photo courtesy of Metro Equipment, Inc., Huntington Beach, CA

Now the salesman had a decision to make. Should he use the automatic scrubber cleaner used in the spot test, or choose the same cleaner, but with a chemical "punch." What would you do? Why not use the stronger of the two? The chemical "punch" could alter the performance in such a way that might not be acceptable. It might create too much foam or eat the rubber bushings and squeegees on their scrubbers. The scrubber cleaner with the "punch" is used for heavy duty floor finish stripping. When in doubt, talk to the chemist that added the chemical punch to your possible test cleaner. The chemist said; "the cleaner with the chemical punch should be OK!"

None of the other competitors pre-tested their cleaners before the big *"Scrub-off."* I guess I wouldn't be telling this story to you, if after all this, he had lost.

The low-foam automatic scrubber cleaner-degreaser with the "punch" won the test and all the flight deck and hangar deck cleaner used for that year amounted to 150 55-gallon drums or nearly $64,000. In addition to that, the USS Coral Sea had *"no incidents"* on their six month cruise, which means nothing slipped off the flight deck and into the ocean due to the decks being kept in a non-slip condition by the salesman's *initiative, desire and experience.* This is a rare case where listening to the car radio news *paid off big.* He wouldn't have found this lead in any directory.

Bob and flight deck cleaner on the USS Coral Sea

This experience led to the salesman (it was me) selling two additional aircraft carriers, the nuclear carriers USS Enterprise and USS Carl Vinson.

The salesman's commission check amount for one order from an aircraft carrier *broke the computer!* The salesmen were paid weekly and the computer was not programmed to issue a five-figure commission check for one week's sales. His commission for that week was over $10,000 and the computer only cut a check for the overage amount. When the "slightly upset" salesman called the company to complain, everybody laughed as no salesman had ever earned over $10,000 in one week! They sent him a hand-written check for the omitted $10,000, overnight. Keep your *eyes* and *ears* and *your imagination open* to these kinds of selling opportunities as *they really pay-off big.*

Thirty-six of 2,000 five-gallon pails of flight deck cleaner being loaded onto the USS Enterprise nuclear aircraft carrier CVN-65

14

Reducing The Odds

1. Warm up Those 'Cold Calls'

If you see a company in your travels that you think might be a potential customer and just go in and use your wits as best as you can, that's a *"cold call."* You have nothing to hang your hat on. You don't know anything about this company, the product or the people. Your percent chance of landing this company as a customer is very, very slim at best and you ruin your reputation for any future consideration. Instead, take note of the prospect and come back after you know more about this company and have thought out and planned your presentation. Armed with your knowledge, call the person who can make a decision to buy and make an appointment. You know who this is because you called and asked or you looked at the company's home page and looked up the officer's names and titles. You have turned this "cold call," equal to the chance of winning the lottery, into a very high percentage presentation to the correct decision making person. If you don't close on the first try, you have made a good, thoughtful presentation and have learned enough about their needs to regroup and now give them exactly what they are looking for. You have converted a low percentage *"cold call"* into a high percentage, intelligent, professional sales presentation. You have a finite number of prospects in your territory. If, in your haste to cover your territory and please your sales manager, you make a lot of *"cold calls"* and very few sales, you are burning your bridges behind you. *Warm up your "cold calls"* and give yourself a chance to make a sale. If you are in a repeat sale business, the extra time you spend preparing will be well worth it for the *business* and *commissions* you will enjoy over and over through the years.

2. First Impressions

If you were a truck mechanic working on the engine in a Kenworth Truck and looked up and saw a man dressed in a Brooks Brother's suit, white shirt and a tie, carrying an attaché case, your first impression would be; "Here comes a city boy who's going to try to sell me something!" Or, "It's a tax man!" "Anyway, I don't trust him!" Your *first impression* can cause negative or positive "vibes" before you open your mouth.

Picture of the Kenworth T2000, Courtesy of Kenworth Truck Company

In this situation, use common sense and take off your coat and tie and roll up your sleeves or wear a short sleeve shirt, preferably blue or a polo shirt. Now your one of them and they will be more likely to talk with you and listen to what you have to say. This has worked very well for me.

If you are selling to a corporation, bank or a facility whose employees wear suits and ties, it is beneficial to your sales presentation that you dress appropriately. These days, many companies have a "business casual" dress code. It is appropriate for you to dress "business casual" if you are required as part of your selling/servicing duties, to do testing or other work related service in the customer's manufacturing plant. If you are making a presentation to the executives of a "business casual" company, you show your respect if you wear a suit and tie. If you are in a hot climate in the summer, it is acceptable to wear a short sleeved white or blue dress shirt and slacks and dress shoes and socks. If no one wears a tie in these conditions, don't wear a tie. Take a tie with you in case an air-conditioned prospect's employees are required to wear ties. You will appear sloppy with no tie in this situation.

If you are selling to the Presidents of corporations or top executives, my favorite outfit would be a navy blue pinned stripe (faint stripes, not bold stripes} two-button or a conservative three-button suit with moderate lapels (not narrow or wide), white or light blue or white with thin dark blue stripes, long sleeve shirt with a modern width tie as recommended by the fine store in which you bought your suit. If you have excellent taste, pick your own tie. The tie shouldn't be too loud or it will distract from your presentation. Please do not try to resurrect your old suit, as it will be out of style and probably doesn't fit that well anymore. *Knowing that you look good gives you great confidence.* Your shoes should be black lace-up or black loafers (not the moccasin type) and navy blue or black stockings. Your black shoes should be shined and the heels should not be worn down. If you come into a presentation looking *well dressed and confident*, you have a much better chance of closing the sale.

Keep yourself as fit and trim as you can to compliment your "corporate look" and your confidence. A black or dark gray suit is also acceptable. Stay away from brown. Always use common sense in considering what to wear depending on the situation. It is always *better to over-dress* for a questionable situation than under-dress. If you buy your clothes from a well-known men's or women's store or a fine department store, they will help you to look your best. Looking good will help you sell, so spend some money on looking good and it will pay you back many times over.

3. Who Has the Authority to Buy?

One thing every salesman should know is that "the buyer" **does not** have any authority to buy! The "buyer" can only process the order when told by someone else in charge of the various departments to order something. It's the *"someone else" we must find and sell.* How do we find the right person? Just ask. You know in your industry the title or titles of the persons that initiate the order, so ask who in this company has that title. If it's a company with which you are not familiar, ask who is in charge of so and so division? The operator or receptionist will often tell you, "Oh, you have to see the buyer." You have to stick to your guns and tell her you always deal with the head engineer or the plant manager and never deal directly with a buyer. What is the plant manager's name and extension number? *You can't afford to let an operator* or receptionist tell *you, a professional salesman, who to see.* You have to *tell her who you want to see!* If you handle her in the right way, she will be glad to give you all the information you need. Some salesmen have a small gift in their case to help them get the full cooperation of a receptionist. It sounds corny, but anything that will get the information you want is worth a try. A receptionist has a boring job. She sees countless salesmen of all calibers and has built up a routine defense against them. If you can *bring a little joy and attention into her life,* she will be a little more likely to help you.

At any rate, you have to find the one person in a corporation who has the *authority to initiate an order* after hearing your presentation. There are a lot of pretenders in every corporation that will gladly listen to your sales pitch, which makes them feel important, and makes 5:00 pm seem to come sooner. The pretender will take the information to the real authority if it will give him points or he will throw your information in the wastebasket and go home. Always make sure you are presenting your product and or service to the *one and only correct person who can make the decision* himself to buy your products, or you are wasting your time.

4. People Knowledge

Selling is money generated and people generated business. We tend to think of the money side, but selling is largely a *"People Business!"*

We think of selling to big corporations and we sell for big corporations. Corporations neither buy nor sell products or services. It is the *people* in both organizations that must come together for their mutual benefit. Corporations don't sell, people do. Corporations don't buy, people do. So people interacting with people, in a business relationship, is the way business and sales get done.

If ten salesmen try to sell their product to a corporate person, why did only one succeed? Nine salesmen didn't fit their product "puzzle piece" exactly into the "puzzle piece opening" in the corporate decision maker's mind. The tenth and successful salesman did his homework and saw what piece was missing, and with a little salesmanship grease, asked if he could complete the puzzle with his piece, and it fit. This salesman may not have the best personality of the ten, or not be the best dressed, or even have the best rapport with the decision maker, but his was the only piece to complete the decision maker's puzzle. *A salesman must find out exactly what the decision maker wants.* One person must ask another person what they want, and then offer it to them. If, in talking to the decision maker he tells you he wants something you don't have but you have something newer and better and you can prove it, your puzzle piece will now fit exactly into his new revised puzzle. It's called people helping people or simply, *"salesmanship."* Remember, corporations don't buy anything but *people do.*

"Selling" is one or more people convincing one or more people to trade their dollars for goods or services that will benefit them more than the value of the dollars. In these days of electronic communication, it is still a *face-to-face, people-to-people* business.

Dilbert ©: Scott Adams/Dist. by United Feature Syndicate, Inc.

15

Secret Weapons

1. A Seldom Used, Under-Utilized Sales Tool

Your sales management! Also, utilize the executives of your company in appropriate situations to close or seal the deal or contract. Use your Sales Manager or Vice President of Sales to help you close a big prospect. They reinforce, in spades, what you have told this prospect about your product, your company and your service. Sales Managers travel all over America and all over the world and they can tell huge success stories of big well-known corporations that are now successfully using your products. They have the authority to negotiate a deal on the spot, right now. They have more experience than you have in dealing and negotiating with big multi-plant corporations. They have earned the right to be the "Sales Manager." *So use them!*

Some or most salesmen misuse their sales management by setting up calls with customers who like them and are very satisfied with the product, service and the sales rep. This is supposed to show the Sales Manager that the sales rep is doing a good job. This is a waste of the Sales Manager's, the customer's and the sales rep's time. The Sales Manager already knows exactly what every sales rep is doing from the sales figures, calls to the office, and the quality and on-time regularity of his sales reports. This is a sign of a sales rep's insecurity. On the other hand, don't take your sales manager on a "cold call" where you have never been and don't know anyone or the situation, hoping he will know how to sell them something. It is bad enough going into a prospect on a "cold call' by yourself knowing nothing and no one and with no appointment, but don't embarrass yourself and your manager with the rejection and indifference you both will have to face.

Properly and most effectively, *bring your Sales Manager into the prospects on which you have been working, know the people, understand their operation and know precisely what you are trying to sell and why.* This strategy will impress your Sales Manager and the prospect and will probably help close the sale. *Run your Sales*

Manager ragged with these kinds of sales calls and you will help yourself accelerate to *the No. 1, money earnings position* in your corporation.

2. Paint a Picture

"Sell the sizzle, not the steak!" Ask questions and *listen* to the prospect's answers and everything he says. He wants the Mercedes or he wouldn't have come in. *He wants to be sold. He needs justification* to pay the price of a Mercedes, but he wants it!

Give him his justification, prestige! *Color* shows he is outgoing. *Image* is important in his work. *German engineering and quality* will last longer and require fewer repairs. Better warranty than all the others because of the quality. Outstanding service with a *no-charge loaner* when service is scheduled. *He will look great and successful to his customers and his friends. High resale value* will cut the total cost of the Mercedes. Your *successful image* will help you in your business to look successful and to be more successful. *"Success breeds success!"* What would a compact car do for your image? What would your friends and customers think about your success? You are buying much more than just reliable transportation. You are buying *style, prestige, success, image, safety and pleasure,* and it is *tax deductible! Just sign here and you can drive your new Mercedes-Benz home now.*

3. Name Dropping

Name-dropping can help close a sale, but be careful as it can be a double-edged sword. You have to consider how the naming of the prospect's arch-competitor as a big customer of yours who sells a lot of the product you are asking them to buy. This can be good, or it can backfire and lose the sale. I would use this only if all other efforts have failed and you have nothing to lose—except any future sales.

Name-dropping can be useful if used with tact and common sense to a smaller prospect that probably admires a large company that is using your product. If you are proud of the fact your company's product or products are being used by a well-known and prominent customer (and you should be), it won't hurt you to mention it to your prospect. What you are saying to the prospect is, "If that wonderful, successful corporation uses my product, it must be good and will benefit you too." Hopefully, you have given the prospect several reasons that your product will benefit them before you feel it necessary or helpful in getting the order.

4. Any Objections

When a prospect raises an objection, you know he has been listening to your presentation. This is a positive sign. Try to *think in advance* what objections may well be either voiced or thought of by your prospects. Also, take mental notes and listen carefully to all objections raised in your sales presentations and think of how you can improve your answers. A professional salesman will *incorporate the answers* to most objections raised *into his presentation* to eliminate any doubts about the benefits the decision maker will receive, *so he has no objection to signing the order.*

"Your price is too high" is probably the most often heard objection. The price your prospect charges for "his" manufactured products are considered high, but he offers a better *overall value* to his customers than his low-priced competitors. The same is true for our product and service, a better value for you than the lower priced brands.

What if you were selling one of the many "low-priced" products? All you have to sell is price and wild claims that your product is better. It won't stand up to a quality brand in *"value added" benefits* to most prospects. Sell your overall *"value added"* benefits and *you will win a very high percentage of the time.* (Please see Chapter 3, No. 1, "Pricing Knowledge," paragraph six, "I am happy", for an outstanding example of how to defeat the price objection.)

16

You're An Actor, So Perform

1. Samples

Salesman's samples are the tools of your trade. Treat them with care as they represent, in the flesh, what you are telling the prospect to expect to receive. If the samples are perfect, it is to your advantage to show them, and, if not they can hurt you. In the apparel industry, the salesman sells with samples of the "new line." They better be pressed and in order of your presentation. Sometimes live models are used and every garment must be laid out in the exact order of your presentation and coordinated with the national marketing plan. If a salesman is selling cars, they should be polished and shiny and the glass sparkling. If selling tricycles, the samples should be oiled to avoid squeaks and simonized to a bright shine. *All your samples should be first class.* If a sample becomes soiled or dented or scratched, order a new one. *Do not try to sell a bent sword.*

In selling bulk toys, if the toy buyer had kids we would offer an appropriate sample toy fire engine or tricycle sample to him at the end of a season, and, if accepted, we would deliver it to his home, personally. It would cost money to ship these bulk toys back to the factory and they were worth far more in appreciation value. Samples are important to your selling success, so always keep them in top condition.

2. Your Vehicle Is A Sales Tool

Your customers see you when you drive into their parking lot. When you take a prospect to lunch, your car is a reflection of you and your work habits. When your up-to-date vehicle is clean and neat with plenty of gas and well organized, they will be favorably impressed that you will attend to detail on their behalf with your service of their account. If your car is dirty and an old McDonald's hamburger carton is sticking out from under the front seat along with a couple of old

French fries, customer sales files all over the back seat and floor, what will your prospect think? Not much of you, your organization or the promised servicing of his account. This salesman's car should be condemned by the health department! After lunch, the prospect will say goodbye at the curb and dash into his company restroom to wash his hands and say to himself; never again. It's not the vehicle that lost the business. It's the sales person's sloppiness, lack of proper attention to his job, lack of organization and a *complete lack of common sales sense and sales aptitude.* This is not the road to No. 1 and the *"Big money"!*

3. A Demonstration Is Worth A Thousand Words

If someone were trying to sell Winchester Rifles or Colt Pistols and in demonstrating their accuracy they missed the bulls eye most of the time, or even once, it appears that there is something wrong with the guns. The *doubt* will force the U. S. Military to look to a competitor who is selling an inferior firearm but has *taught himself to shoot straight.* Millions of dollars lost because the salesman didn't practice or hire a championship marksman for the *most important demonstration of his lifetime.*

Demonstrations are the proof that what you say is true. It is more than that, *it is showmanship!* Always prepare before you demonstrate your product for a prospective customer. Check your equipment. Apologies during a "demo" won't fly and you will lose the opportunity. Practice on smaller customers before fumbling in front of a major prospect. *"Play Philadelphia before you hit Broadway!"* After a few demos, you will get all of the mistakes out of your system and gain some new ideas and the *confidence* you need to demonstrate your product or system to the big ones. The successful demos will reinforce your knowledge and enthusiasm about your product.

Use common sense, *observe the situation* and make any adjustments necessary to give you and your product a fighting chance. Remember, you're fighting the resistance to change in all humans and *"Murphy's Law."* "What can go wrong, will." Someone once failed to check the connection on a high-pressure hose and metal wand which blew off and knocked a worker off of the wing of an aircraft. Luckily, he was saved by a safety harness, but the potential sale was lost. I will bet that every salesman has at least one demo disaster to tell. One is admissible as the first try in front of a prospect is in uncharted waters. Learn, and move on. You will get better the more demos you do, and when the demos result in orders and commissions, you'll love them.

One demonstration to a major truck line of aluminum brightener, where the aluminum trailers are pulled through an automatic truck wash, resulted in a 100 55-gallon drum order and a new customer. The aluminum brightener the trucking company had been using was from a major nationally known chemical company, and probably is just as good as the one demonstrated. Common sense and product knowledge gained from many previous demos stacked the deck in the demonstrating salesman's favor to win. There were two drive-through wash racks. After observing the operation in action for a few minutes, it was obvious that one wash rack was doing a much better job than the other. The most efficient rack was chosen for the test. It was also observed that the driver who pulled the trailers through the wash rack was driving through too fast to give the brightener a chance to work efficiently. All chemical cleaners, and especially aluminum brighteners, need time to work. In addition, heat helps as acid-based cleaners double in strength with every 20 degree rise in temperature. These racks mixed the brightener with cold water so more time was needed for the brightener to work properly. *The driver was asked to drive through much more slowly to give the cleaner a chance* to do a better job on the trailers. *That was the key!* Also, opening up the metering device to allow a greater mixture ratio of brightener to the *cold* water to help it perform better during the test was critical to the outstanding result. Setting up and *controlling the test* to give your product every possible advantage comes from experience. You already know from previous demonstrations of this product what it takes to produce an absolutely beautifully brightened aluminum truck trailer. You must see that the conditions for your very important demonstration are set up *to give your product every advantage over your competitor.*

Bob Felgen demonstrating aluminum brightener

The principal was told the set-up and test would take some time and he would be called when the test was complete. With the few adjustments, the demonstration was extremely successful. The boss was called to see the results. There were several dirty, streaked trailers partially cleaned with the competitor's brightener on the rack with clogged nozzles and a quick drive through and weak solution, done before our test was started. There were also several bright, shiny trailers with no streaks that were the test trailers, and after talking to the yard driver as to which were the test trailers, there was absolutely no doubt which was the better aluminum brightener.. Those few simple observations and adjustments before the demonstration insured a winning *$40,000 order* in less than an hour after the results were seen. With the same adjustments, the competitive brightener would have worked just as well. *Smart demonstrations bring in new business, big commissions and it counts as a big sales increase*

Competitive Aluminum Brightener

Winning Test Aluminum Brightener

17

Be A Patron Of The Arts

1. The Art of Asking Questions

Asking questions is the best way to work your way through the maze of what is in the prospect's mind.

- What does he or she like?

- What don't they like?

- What are they looking for?

- What are you doing now?

- Are you the person to whom I should be talking?

- What performance are you getting from the unit you are now using?

- Are you completely satisfied with the current vendor's service?

- Would you be interested if I told you how my company's product and service are going to greatly increase your productivity and profits?

- Will you please sign this order?

There is no value in asking questions if you don't *really listen*. The answers may change your next question if you listen carefully to the answers they give you. Most salesmen think to be a good salesman they should talk and the prospect should listen. If the prospect doesn't talk or you don't listen, how can you know what the prospect is thinking? *Selling is a two-way street*. If you don't ask questions, and the prospect never says a word, it is like no applause between jokes of a stand-up comedian. The sales rep has a good chance of getting no applause after his presentation if he doesn't include the prospect in the process. What would have happened if you hadn't asked your wife the most important question, "Will you marry me?" Don't answer that!

2. The Art of Listening

It should be called *"the art of paying attention."* As a professional salesman, do you always, or do you ever, remember the person's name after he or she gives it to you? Most of us don't. We are too busy thinking about what we want to say. At the end of the conversation we usually say, "It was nice meeting you?" Or, sheepishly, "What was your name again?"

A salesman has a story about his or her product to tell. They tell it many times, hopefully improving as they go along, so it is natural to want to get their company's money's worth and get the whole story out on every sales presentation. If a prospect interrupts to make a point or ask a question, stop and *pay attention* to what he is saying as you may have to go to "Plan B" and answer his question and continue on. His question shows his interest in what you are saying and his questions, if you really listen, are telling you what he is thinking. There is nothing worse than no questions or comments through the entire presentation and a, "Thank you, I'll think about it, goodbye." It's like no applause at the end of a Broadway musical. After the first act, maybe *the rep should start asking the questions.* No use becoming a good listener if the presentation doesn't spark some questions and some back and forth conversation that leads you closer to *applause at the end in the form of an order.*

Where good listening pays off big during a presentation is when you hear and recognize an opportunity for a *"trial close."* When a prospect says something that indicated to you he is interested or is agreeing with what you are saying, *stop* in the middle of your presentation *and ask him or her to place an order.* Robot reps don't hear or recognize buyer acceptance and are hell-bent to finish their complete presentation—and lose the order. I call it *"slacking the line"* by not sinking the hook when the buyer obviously is on the hook. By finishing the whole story, the fish gets bored and swims away. Many people in sales have *lost many sales by talking too much instead of listening more.*

3. Gifts: The Art of Showing Genuine Appreciation

Most companies and corporations have a "no gifts" policy in force. Corporate officers don't want a gift to wrongly influence a buying decision. A corporation employs thousands of workers far removed from the corporate officers. Some are dissatisfied, passed over and under paid, and are eager to accept gifts as due retribution for their dead-end situation. Others have created their own little dynasty within the corporation that they rule. They might be unashamed or even eager to accept a gift, if offered. If this is a department that uses your type of products and you haven't gotten anywhere with your salesmanship, look around and the rep will probably see several items that bear a competitor's name. This is a good indication he accepts things from the competition. A salesman can do two things. You can give him a company pen, paper weight or baseball cap, which indicates you are a "giver." Ask for an order and see what happens. The other action a rep can take in this situation is to thank the man for listening, give him your card and leave, forever. This guy will buy a little bit from everybody and end up buying from the rep that gives him the most, until someone else gives him more. Walk away, your selling time is too valuable to waste on this impossible situation. Come to think of it, there is a third choice. The rep has nothing to lose to go to someone higher up in the organization if he thinks it's worth his time.

Like entertainment, giving gifts, once started, can never be stopped and it is dangerous to make the gift smaller than the last one. Some corporations, if not most, send notices before Christmas to their vendors telling them that their employees are not allowed to accept gifts.

A professional salesman knows his big customers very well. He has a feel for when and to whom it is appropriate to give a gift as a *"thank you"* for the business received that year. What kind of gift? Something in good taste and in line with the amount of business received. Your sales manager can make un-official suggestions as he deals with all the sales reps and will know what the successful ones give in your type of business. You can give a two-pound box of the best candy in town. A canned ham or a Butterball Turkey or a bottle of booze is OK, if you know what kind and brand they like. For instance, if a good customer drinks Dewar's Scotch when you have entertained him in the evening, (you should have made a note of this on your account sheet in your planner) buy a *quart or "half gallon"* (1.75 liters) for him in a Christmas box as a "thank you" for the business relationship you have enjoyed this past year.

This book is about "Selling Secrets that Show you the Money." So, I'll tell it like it really is. In all of my many years as a professional "Outside Salesman," *a gift at Christmas time was always well received and appreciated.* Only once in all those years did one person politely refuse to accept a gift at Christmas to show my appreciation for his business. I told him I understood and gave the gift to another customer. If you are on commission, the cost of these business gifts is tax deductible. If on an expense account, you will have a budget limit to cover the cost. If you were in a position to authorize buying supplies for your company from several similar suppliers, what if only one appreciated your business enough to say thank you with a small gift? *You will get more business next year than your competitors who honored "the letter." Let common sense and the understanding of human nature guide you.*

18

Open The Right Door, Then "Close" It

1. 'Closing' (Asking For The Order!)

After giving an outstanding presentation of your products and services, there is that *"pause"* when *you must be quick to "ask for the order."* Otherwise, you will hear that all too familiar indecisive reply; *"Let me think about it."* It is human nature to be indecisive about making a decision. You must help him over the hump and reinforce the benefits he will reap by saying yes to your order. You know he is going to hesitate, so *beat him to the punch* and reinforce his reasons that benefit him and *make him a hero* to give you the *order now.* Then get the hell out of there before he changes his mind. Let him "think about it" all he wants to after you are miles away *with the signed order in your hand.*

Let's say you are a nice guy and let him think about it for a day or two and arrange to meet with him again in a few days. *You have already lost the order.* Ninety-nine point nine percent of the time he has had time to reinforce his doubts and is comfortable with the status quo, and you haven't been in on the decision this time. Another scenario that can happen if you *"slack the line"* in closing the order in this situation is the competitor who comes in after you have left, makes a similar presentation asks for the order before the prospect has a chance to "think about it," reinforces the benefits and hands the order and a pen to the prospect, and the order is signed. Even if a salesman makes a logical presentation, that is only a part of the total process of inducing a prospect to any action. *You* must tell him what he should do to make all these wonderful things you talked about happen. *You ask him to sign the order* or make out a purchase order while you are there and you will see that is processed immediately.

2. Double Your Orders

If you are selling almost anything, you can double your "fill-in order" by having a *pre-written promotional order*, coordinated with national advertising, in your coat pocket to be presented to the buyer *after the fill-in order has been written and signed.* It's a quick sale and will double your fill-in order. *It should be thought out and written the night before your sales call.* This is one of the strategies that separate the successful salesmen from the average salesmen.

I was selling a high-fashion line of bras and girdles in North and South Dakota, Montana and Wyoming. I would travel from town to town, taking inventory of my brand and then writing a "fill-in order" to replace the sizes that were missing. I wrote fill-in orders all across this vast territory. This isn't sales-manship. Anyone can do this. I was a good driver and a good counter, but I haven't *sold* anything.

I drove into Aberdeen, South Dakota one evening as I had a couple of custom-ers I will be seeing in the morning. My territory was a "training territory" and I was under pressure (my own) to sell myself into a major market territory and fill-ins wouldn't cut it. My company was high fashion and sent its designers to Paris each season to see what the Paris fashion industry was offering for the next sea-son. The designers would then come out with high fashion bras and under gar-ments to go with the new Paris fashions.

Common sense would tell us that the women in the Dakotas, Montana and Wyoming could care less about the skinny, exotic high-fashion creations sold In Paris and New York. All my company's advertising was in high fashion magazines such as Vogue, Harpers Bazaar, Ladies Home Journal and many others.

So my burning desire forced me to try something that could be considered salesmanship and that night I pulled out a co-op advertising "ad mat" of the new-est Paris fashion coordinated "Merry Widow" type garment called the "Philly." The "Philly" was designed for a woman with an "hour-glass figure" and had fancy lace and blue ribbons and bows. I haven't seen any "hour glass figures" since I took this territory. This was an extremely expensive garment.

I wrote an order that night large enough to qualify for co-op advertising and presented it after I wrote the fill-in order. To my amazement the intimate apparel buyer liked the *idea* of the high fashion image it would give her store and with a window display of the garment along with an ad in their local newspaper (50 per-cent paid by my company) and timed to match the national magazines full page ads of the garment called "Philly." This was an extra order that more than dou-bled my fill-in order and more than that, it created excitement with the buyer and now I could consider myself a salesman. I did this everywhere and this promotional idea using various products was responsible for doubling my sales and a promotion to a major territory.

In the chemical industry and other industries, orders can be increased and the salesman will be thanked. With the announcement of a forthcoming price increase, sell your customers on stocking extra inventory before the increase takes affect. This will free your time to make more prospect presentations as they won't need a fill-in for some time and a competitor can't slip in a trial order because your customer is "loaded."

As soon as I found out a product of mine, that one of my biggest customers used, had been banned from being manufactured, I immediately contacted the customer and wrote an order for the entire inventory that was on hand in all of our manufacturing plants. These are the opportunities, if realized, that make the difference in the race to the top, not to mention the *extra* money.

I heard that one of my biggest airplane manufacturers was going to hold an "open-house for their airline and military customers. I immediately called my contacts in Facility Maintenance and suggested a new coat of sealer be applied to the production and assembly floors so it would look its best for this important occasion. That turned out to be a $30,000 sales call. A salesman has to be creative and help his or her customers become heroes. Their facility looked great for the "Open House" for their prospects and customers. Facility Maintenance Department got the credit and I got the money.

19

Dollars At The Finish Line

1. 'All Work and No Play'

All the chapters in this book tell a salesman how to be successful in his profession. *There is the other side of the coin. Think about your family.* The outside salesman, to be successful, must be away from home days and sometimes weeks at a time. With the planning time on weekends and when you are in town, you are gone all day, every day. When you get home, a salesman must take an hour to plan for the next day's sales calls.

Put yourself in your wife's place. She is alone most of the time, except for the kids. If your wife works and you have no children, she is busy at work during the day, but alone at night when her husband is on the road. When you are in town, the evenings are short and you have to steal an hour of it to plan for tomorrow. Would you trade places with her? The answer is no.

Do not waste those precious hours and weekends with your wife and kids. They have been waiting all week or all day for their husband and father to come home. As in the field with your customers, *stay positive and cheerful.* While planning, plan some special activity for your family that will be fun and something good to think of when you are not there.

If your work demands are explained to your family and you pay full attention to your family when you are with them, everything will turn out fine. *This is not a "normal" family situation and it needs extra special attention from a professional salesman.*

2. Financial Considerations

Most professional salesmen know the story *"Death of a Salesman"* by Arthur Miller. The star salesman was fired by the founder's young son who had just taken-over the family business. The generation gap erased any understanding or consideration of his long years as a good sales representative for his father. *At an advanced age, he was out of work and on the street for the first time in his life.* He was always the father's favorite and *thought he would work for the company until he wanted to retire.*

These days, with all the mergers taking place, this story is told over and over. It's not the young son, but the army of managers who, for economy and to please the stock holders, *lay-off most of the sales force* of the company being bought and replace them with their own salesmen, now selling both company's products. *Now you are a lot older and just starting another sales job.*

The story of *"The Ant and the Grasshopper"* also applies. The ants worked hard all summer gathering food for the winter, while the grasshopper played. When winter came, the grasshopper was out in the cold and starving while the ants were warm and safe from the elements, and had plenty of food. This is a story I was told when I was young and indestructible and I didn't get it! *Now I fully understand its lesson. Some of us are like the grasshopper, I am afraid.*

Major League pitchers and hitters are considered *too old* to produce *when they reach forty. Airline pilots are retired at age sixty* and *sales representatives in their fifties find it much harder to find the sales job they want or keep the one they have.* So, it would be wise to *look ahead to that time. Save, invest and buy real estate while you are young* so you can enjoy an early retirement *if you want to, or have to.*

Retirement is not what you think it will be like. After a few months, the garage is clean and organized, you have taken a few trips and gained a few pounds, and there is not much to do. Even if you play golf, your life is somewhat empty and you may find *you miss the challenge, the money and being important* to a top corporation and *to yourself.*

After a lifetime of interacting with your customer friends and company "teammates" and *out-selling your competitors*, believe it or not, *you will miss the great feeling of being important and being able to do more for your loved ones financially.*

Modern medicine is finding ways to enable us to extend our lives. Life expectancy after retirement age is currently 17 years. If you don't want to live like the grasshopper and for a longer percentage of your life, do some thinking outside the sales box and *create a worry-free financial life for yourself and your family.* If necessary and it probably will be, hire a financial advisor to help choose the best funds in your company's 401(k) that will give you the best return. *By paying attention to your investment by hiring a professional, you will retire with significantly more money than you will if you don't pay attention.* Remember, all withdrawals are taxable. Withdrawals before age 59½ carry a penalty of 10 percent of the withdrawal amount plus tax. *Withdrawals really cripple the growth and final amount at retirement. You lose the compound interest* while you are paying back the loan. If it is a *"hardship,"* which you don't pay back, *you rob your retirement of the loan amount and the compound interest on that amount over the many years before you retire.*

It's tempting to know you have a chunk of money you can get your hands on to buy that new car or a down payment on a bigger, more prestigious house or for the kid's college, but *consider the 401(k) "untouchable!"* You will be glad you let it *grow, untouched,* when you retire and find you have *one million dollars* instead of $35,000, *less tax.* Forget Social Security. Don't count on it. If it's still there when you retire, consider it a small monthly bonus for all the money you put into it while you were working. It's not enough on which to retire and it may not even be there by the time you retire. *Spend a little of that sales planning time on your future financial security, as airline pilots and sports stars aren't the only ones who get retired early.*

3. It Seems As Far Away As Pluto

Many professional salesmen have earned a lot of money during their prime selling years. Sales commissions and bonuses were substantial and we lived well. *Invest the money from the good times.* You will need at least *two pensions plus other substantial investments to be able to retire* (a bad word) *with the same income or more than your current yearly income. People live longer now* and to finally retire and *spend 20+ years without income, except for Social Security, is not a pretty picture.* Look at *Social Security,* if it is still there by the time you retire, as *grocery money.* It won't cover the house payment or rent, health care, travel, hobbies, insurance, vehicles and all the other things that require money.

When we are young we want a lot of "things." We want to impress our friends and neighbors. I talk from experience. I always had the best car of all my friends. *My friends are mostly dead and the car dealers have retired on my money. Don't spend it! Invest it! Make your money work for you* making more money. Vehicles and other "things" are *"Black Holes"* where your money goes in and never comes out! Of course you have to have a vehicle to live and to do your work, but you don't have to have a Porsche Carrera GT!

The sales profession is a minefield for financial disaster. Variable income, job changes, long overnight trips away from home, divorces, mergers and many other obstacles to financial security. My advice is to find and hire a good legitimate nationally-known financial investment corporation and invest as much of your income as possible on a regular schedule. Diversify your investments and avoid the too-good-to-be-true "hot deals!"

At age 55, when the merger reorganization has no place for you after 30 or more successful years and you are financially independent, you will be glad you have your investments. If you think of yourself in this situation, living for each paycheck to pay bills with little or no savings, you will start investing now, while you are young or even older than young, as much of each paycheck as possible toward your *"Independence Day."* You can get used to living with 85 percent or even 80 percent of your sales earnings. *Let 15 to 20 percent of your money be working for you on the side, like a silent partner.* You are, faster than you realize, approaching 20 or more years of retirement without any income except Social Security, which is not enough. *Live like a king now, and suffer greatly later, when you can't afford anything!* It's up to you **now** to decide *how you will live the last 20 years of your life.*

If you are wise and think about the time when you will be too old to work, you will start right now to invest at least *ten percent or more* of your earnings every month of every year of your selling career. (As of 2007, the financial experts are telling workers they must invest at least 17 percent of their income and to get professional help on how to invest and grow that money so you and your family will be able retire with dignity.)

Ninety percent of $60,000 is $54,000 on which to live now. Ten percent is $6,000 per year to invest *to work like a silent partner* for you and your family, on the side, for your own future security and peace of mind. When you invest $6,000 per year at an average return of 7 percent interest, compounded for twenty years, you will have earned $134,791 interest for a grand total of $263,191. Compound $6,000 for thirty years and you will earn $413,838 interest for a total of $606,438.

If you don't make a plan and stick to it, you and your family will most probably retire with only Social Security, a few thousand dollars of 401(k) money, *which is now taxable,* and possibly an IRA or a T-bill worth about $20,000. You will have your house, but you must live somewhere. You will be used to earning $60,000 to $100,000 or more every year. When you retire, your income will be $20,000 from Social Security, you will be taxed on your 401(k) withdrawals and your $20,000 is a one-time emergency use fund which will only last one year eight months at $1,000 per month. To live like you are used to living all your working life and live the last twenty or thirty years at least comfortably and independently, *you need to plan ahead.*

If you are in the $100,000 commission bracket, 10 percent, or $10,000, per year invested at 7 percent compounded for twenty years will earn $224,652 interest for a total of $438,652. *Thirty years* earns $689,730 interest for a grand total of *$1,010,730; "Independence Day!"* (See compound interest charts that follow.)

Compound Interest Charts

Assumptions Used			Your Contributions	Investment Return	Compound Interest	Annual Total	Account Balance
Annual Contribution	$6,000.00	Year 1	$6,000.00	$420.00		$6,420.00	$6,420.00
Investment Return	7%	Year 2	$6,000.00	$420.00	$449.40	$6,869.40	$13,289.40
Twenty years		Year 3	$6,000.00	$420.00	$930.26	$7,350.26	$20,639.66
		Year 4	$6,000.00	$420.00	$1,444.78	$7,864.78	$28,504.43
		Year 5	$6,000.00	$420.00	$1,995.31	$8,415.31	$36,919.74
		Year 6	$6,000.00	$420.00	$2,584.38	$9,004.38	$45,924.13
		Year 7	$6,000.00	$420.00	$3,214.69	$9,634.69	$55,558.82
		Year 8	$6,000.00	$420.00	$3,889.12	$10,309.12	$65,867.93
		Year 9	$6,000.00	$420.00	$4,610.76	$11,030.76	$76,898.69
		Year 10	$6,000.00	$420.00	$5,382.91	$11,802.91	$88,701.60
		Year 11	$6,000.00	$420.00	$6,209.11	$12,629.11	$101,330.71
		Year 12	$6,000.00	$420.00	$7,093.15	$13,513.15	$114,843.86
		Year 13	$6,000.00	$420.00	$8,039.07	$14,459.07	$129,302.93
		Year 14	$6,000.00	$420.00	$9,051.20	$15,471.20	$144,774.13
		Year 15	$6,000.00	$420.00	$10,134.19	$16,554.19	$161,328.32
		Year 16	$6,000.00	$420.00	$11,292.98	$17,712.98	$179,041.30
		Year 17	$6,000.00	$420.00	$12,532.89	$18,952.89	$197,994.20
		Year 18	$6,000.00	$420.00	$13,859.59	$20,279.59	$218,273.79
		Year 19	$6,000.00	$420.00	$15,279.17	$21,699.17	$239,972.95
		Year 20	$6,000.00	$420.00	$16,798.11	$23,218.11	$263,191.06
		Totals	$120,000.00	$8,400.00	$134,791.06	**$263,191.06**	

		Your Contributions	Investment Return	Compound Interest	Annual Total	Account Balance
Assumptions Used						
Annual Contribution	$6,000.00	Year 1	$6,000.00	$420.00		$6,420.00	$6,420.00
Investment Return	7%	Year 2	$6,000.00	$420.00	$449.40	$6,869.40	$13,289.40
Thirty years		Year 3	$6,000.00	$420.00	$930.26	$7,350.26	$20,639.66
		Year 4	$6,000.00	$420.00	$1,444.78	$7,864.78	$28,504.43
		Year 5	$6,000.00	$420.00	$1,995.31	$8,415.31	$36,919.74
		Year 6	$6,000.00	$420.00	$2,584.38	$9,004.38	$45,924.13
		Year 7	$6,000.00	$420.00	$3,214.69	$9,634.69	$55,558.82
		Year 8	$6,000.00	$420.00	$3,889.12	$10,309.12	$65,867.93
		Year 9	$6,000.00	$420.00	$4,610.76	$11,030.76	$76,898.69
		Year 10	$6,000.00	$420.00	$5,382.91	$11,802.91	$88,701.60
		Year 11	$6,000.00	$420.00	$6,209.11	$12,629.11	$101,330.71
		Year 12	$6,000.00	$420.00	$7,093.15	$13,513.15	$114,843.86
		Year 13	$6,000.00	$420.00	$8,039.07	$14,459.07	$129,302.93
		Year 14	$6,000.00	$420.00	$9,051.20	$15,471.20	$144,774.13
		Year 15	$6,000.00	$420.00	$10,134.19	$16,554.19	$161,328.32
		Year 16	$6,000.00	$420.00	$11,292.98	$17,712.98	$179,041.30
		Year 17	$6,000.00	$420.00	$12,532.89	$18,952.89	$197,994.20
		Year 18	$6,000.00	$420.00	$13,859.59	$20,279.59	$218,273.79
		Year 19	$6,000.00	$420.00	$15,279.17	$21,699.17	$239,972.95
		Year 20	$6,000.00	$420.00	$16,798.11	$23,218.11	$263,191.06
		Year 21	$6,000.00	$420.00	$18,423.37	$24,843.37	$288,034.43
		Year 22	$6,000.00	$420.00	$20,162.41	$26,582.41	$314,616.85
		Year 23	$6,000.00	$420.00	$22,023.18	$28,443.18	$343,060.02
		Year 24	$6,000.00	$420.00	$24,014.20	$30,434.20	$373,494.23
		Year 25	$6,000.00	$420.00	$26,144.60	$32,564.60	$406,058.82
		Year 26	$6,000.00	$420.00	$28,424.12	$34,844.12	$440,902.94
		Year 27	$6,000.00	$420.00	$30,863.21	$37,283.21	$478,186.15
		Year 28	$6,000.00	$420.00	$33,473.03	$39,893.03	$518,079.18
		Year 29	$6,000.00	$420.00	$36,265.54	$42,685.54	$560,764.72
		Year 30	$6,000.00	$420.00	$39,253.53	$45,673.53	$606,438.25
		Totals	$180,000.00	$12,600.00	$413,838.25	**$606,438.25**	

Assumptions Used			Your Contributions	Investment Return	Compound Interest	Annual Total	Account Balance
Annual Contribution	$10,000.00	Year 1	$10,000.00	$700.00		$10,700.00	$10,700.00
Investment Return	7%	Year 2	$10,000.00	$700.00	$749.00	$11,449.00	$22,149.00
Twenty years		Year 3	$10,000.00	$700.00	$1,550.43	$12,250.43	$34,399.43
		Year 4	$10,000.00	$700.00	$2,407.96	$13,107.96	$47,507.39
		Year 5	$10,000.00	$700.00	$3,325.52	$14,025.52	$61,532.91
		Year 6	$10,000.00	$700.00	$4,307.30	$15,007.30	$76,540.21
		Year 7	$10,000.00	$700.00	$5,357.81	$16,057.81	$92,598.03
		Year 8	$10,000.00	$700.00	$6,481.86	$17,181.86	$109,779.89
		Year 9	$10,000.00	$700.00	$7,684.59	$18,384.59	$128,164.48
		Year 10	$10,000.00	$700.00	$8,971.51	$19,671.51	$147,835.99
		Year 11	$10,000.00	$700.00	$10,348.52	$21,048.52	$168,884.51
		Year 12	$10,000.00	$700.00	$11,821.92	$22,521.92	$191,406.43
		Year 13	$10,000.00	$700.00	$13,398.45	$24,098.45	$215,504.88
		Year 14	$10,000.00	$700.00	$15,085.34	$25,785.34	$241,290.22
		Year 15	$10,000.00	$700.00	$16,890.32	$27,590.32	$268,880.54
		Year 16	$10,000.00	$700.00	$18,821.64	$29,521.64	$298,402.17
		Year 17	$10,000.00	$700.00	$20,888.15	$31,588.15	$329,990.33
		Year 18	$10,000.00	$700.00	$23,099.32	$33,799.32	$363,789.65
		Year 19	$10,000.00	$700.00	$25,465.28	$36,165.28	$399,954.92
		Year 20	$10,000.00	$700.00	$27,996.84	$38,696.84	$438,651.77
		Totals	$200,000.00	$14,000.00	$224,651.77	$438,651.77	

Assumptions Used			Your Contributions	Investment Return	Compound Interest	Annual Total	Account Balance
Annual Contribution	$10,000.00	Year 1	$10,000.00	$700.00		$10,700.00	$10,700.00
Investment Return	7%	Year 2	$10,000.00	$700.00	$749.00	$11,449.00	$22,149.00
thirty years		Year 3	$10,000.00	$700.00	$1,550.43	$12,250.43	$34,399.43
		Year 4	$10,000.00	$700.00	$2,407.96	$13,107.96	$47,507.39
		Year 5	$10,000.00	$700.00	$3,325.52	$14,025.52	$61,532.91
		Year 6	$10,000.00	$700.00	$4,307.30	$15,007.30	$76,540.21
		Year 7	$10,000.00	$700.00	$5,357.81	$16,057.81	$92,598.03
		Year 8	$10,000.00	$700.00	$6,481.86	$17,181.86	$109,779.89
		Year 9	$10,000.00	$700.00	$7,684.59	$18,384.59	$128,164.48
		Year 10	$10,000.00	$700.00	$8,971.51	$19,671.51	$147,835.99
		Year 11	$10,000.00	$700.00	$10,348.52	$21,048.52	$168,884.51
		Year 12	$10,000.00	$700.00	$11,821.92	$22,521.92	$191,406.43
		Year 13	$10,000.00	$700.00	$13,398.45	$24,098.45	$215,504.88
		Year 14	$10,000.00	$700.00	$15,085.34	$25,785.34	$241,290.22
		Year 15	$10,000.00	$700.00	$16,890.32	$27,590.32	$268,880.54
		Year 16	$10,000.00	$700.00	$18,821.64	$29,521.64	$298,402.17
		Year 17	$10,000.00	$700.00	$20,888.15	$31,588.15	$329,990.33
		Year 18	$10,000.00	$700.00	$23,099.32	$33,799.32	$363,789.65
		Year 19	$10,000.00	$700.00	$25,465.28	$36,165.28	$399,954.92
		Year 20	$10,000.00	$700.00	$27,996.84	$38,696.84	$438,651.77
		Year 21	$10,000.00	$700.00	$30,705.62	$41,405.62	$480,057.39
		Year 22	$10,000.00	$700.00	$33,604.02	$44,304.02	$524,361.41
		Year 23	$10,000.00	$700.00	$36,705.30	$47,405.30	$571,766.71
		Year 24	$10,000.00	$700.00	$40,023.67	$50,723.67	$622,490.38
		Year 25	$10,000.00	$700.00	$43,574.33	$54,274.33	$676,764.70
		Year 26	$10,000.00	$700.00	$47,373.53	$58,073.53	$734,838.23
		Year 27	$10,000.00	$700.00	$51,438.68	$62,138.68	$796,976.91
		Year 28	$10,000.00	$700.00	$55,788.38	$66,488.38	$863,465.29
		Year 29	$10,000.00	$700.00	$60,442.57	$71,142.57	$934,607.86
		Year 30	$10,000.00	$700.00	$65,422.55	$76,122.55	$1,010,730.41
		Totals	$300,000.00	$21,000.00	$689,730.41	$1,010,730.41	

Courtesy of Inmagine Corporation LLC

Plan for One Million Dollars at the Finish Line.

On the other hand, *credit card interest* is about 21 percent on the money you "borrow." *You only get 7 percent for saving, but lose 21 percent, or three times your interest on investments, when you charge purchases on a credit card and don't pay it off each month.* Keep one or two credit cards for convenience or emergencies or car rentals that require a credit card, but *pay the balance in full each month* to avoid paying that killer interest. Multiple credit cards charged to the hilt will divert all your money earmarked for investment and your future well-being *to pay interest only for most of the rest of your life.* It is crazy and dumb to earn 7 percent on your investments and turn around and pay 21 percent every month on the credit card balance, which can be as big as the salesman's total investments. The sales rep will have to sell more and more to keep up with his interest payments. *He may find himself losing sales as he becomes more desperate and "pushy" in his sales approach.*

Professional salesmen should *get rid of those credit cards and the worry* so they can be happy, enthusiastic, optimistic and confident in the knowledge that they are not harming their present and future financial condition. *It is very hard to concentrate on all that is involved in selling, when a salesman is burdened by heavy financial worries. Credit cards are the "Black Holes" of financial progress* and present and future security and peace of mind. Get away from those *"Black Holes"* before they suck you into paying interest only and nothing on reducing principal for the rest of your life. This is one of the *"mines" in the minefield that successful salesmen have to avoid.*

Make sure all interest is flowing into your future and not out. Compound interest is like magic. Start enjoying its benefits at as young an age as you can. Also, if your company offers a *401(k) plan,* and matches your contribution, *take full advantage of it, as their match is free money and your contribution is with pre-tax dollars.* Pay attention to your 401K investments to make sure your 401K money is invested in the most profitable funds. As most professional salesmen are not financial professionals, hire one to suggest the current funds that have the highest percent returns for your 401K investments. You pay taxes at a lower rate, in most cases, when you are retired. The 401K plan was not meant to replace your company's traditional pension plan, but that is what is happening today! Your 401K plan alone won't be enough! You will need other investments such as real estate or investments your financial advisor suggests.

Also look to see if you are eligible for a "Roth IRA." After tax money is invested in a "Roth." Therefore, you pay no tax on your principal or interest earned when you cash out after you are retired. Check the rules and whether it will benefit you with your financial advisor. *You will need everything you have invested when your income is ZERO!*

You may need a new mind-set. Think of your sales profession as your *"second job"* which is feeding money into your *"primary job"* which is investing in your future security and life style.

The average life expectancy today, in 2007, after retirement at age sixty-seven, is seventeen years. It will be longer when you retire. If you earn $75,000 each year and retire today, you will need seventeen times $75,000 or $1,275,000 to be at the same comfort level as when you were working. It is something to think about.

20

To Do Or Not To Do,
This Is The Answer

1. Selling In A Nutshell

The following comprise *selling secrets* to your financial security, in a nutshell.

1.   Ask for the order.

2.   Complete product knowledge.

3.   Complete pricing knowledge.

4.   A burning desire.

5.   Competitive spirit.

6.   Become "Street Smart."

7.   Motivation.

8.   Organization.

9.   Planning.

10. Record keeping.

11. Prioritize your time.

12. Hard work—put in the time.

13. Positive attitude.

14. Persistence.

15. Determination.

16. ***Prospecting.***

17. Common Sense.

18. Enthusiasm.

19. Ingenuity.

20. Ideas.

21. Asking questions.

22. Listening.

23. Extra presentations.

24. Demonstrate.

25. "Sell the Sizzle."

26. Know your competition.

27. Work smart.

28. Minimize distractions.

29. Dress appropriately.

30. Develop sales radar to "see" extra opportunities.

31. Save and invest for your future.

2. Things to Avoid In the Minefield of Selling

To be successful and financially independent, these are the things to avoid in the "minefield of selling."

1. Failing to ask for the order.

2. Don't run around your territory with your plans down. Plan and prioritize.

3. Never give up.

4. Do not let yourself be distracted.

5. Do not make a promise unless you can keep it.

6. Don't watch everything on TV; they are getting paid, you are not.

7. Don't express your views on politics, religion or sex with a customer or prospect.

8. Do not discuss what another customer is doing that would give away a competitive advantage.

9. Don't listen to your car radio all the time. You spend much of your selling time in your car, so turn off the radio and think about your next call.

10. Don't be lazy or sloppy in getting your sales reports done right and in on time. This gives the sales manager a picture of the salesman's attitude and work ethic.

11. Don't demonstrate unless you know what you are doing and arrange the components of a demonstration to ensure a successful outcome.

12. Avoid telling jokes.

13. Do not lie.

14. Do not bad-mouth your competitors. He or she might be a buyer's good friend. Stick to selling your own products and you will become a friend too.

15. Don't quit early. Most competitors will.

16. Do not be late for an appointment.

17. Do not make a fine presentation to the wrong person.

18. Do not make a weak presentation to the right person.

19. Do not make wild claims.

20. Avoid using the word "fantastic."

21. Don't over sell and under prove.

22. Do not smoke while talking to a prospect or customer.

23. Do not be unfaithful when on the road. Nothing destroys a salesman's attention to business more than a divorce. This is the ultimate distraction.

24. Don't let yourself get discouraged. Your family and your company are depending on you.

25. Don't ever forget about *"Financial Independence Day."* Save and invest now so you will be able to enjoy your later years with dignity.

    Will you be independent by the fourth quarter of your life? Or will you have to work *overtime*? (Not at "time and one half", but at about *half* your average working year's income.) It's something to think about *now*!

21

Marketing, Factory Reps Or Distributors

1. Distributor Salesmen

Salesmen that sell for a distributor sell products manufactured by many different companies. Some large distributors in the chemical industry manufacture some products and compete with some name brands they also sell. Distributor salesmen cover much smaller territories, usually a small section of a city with street boundaries on four sides. Some distributors have catalogues of products, usually covering one industry, that are as big as the Los Angeles telephone book. Distributor salesmen territories are close to the distributors office and warehouse and the salesman's home. Some distributors' salesmen are required to come in to process their orders every day for an hour from 4:00 to 5:00 pm. Usually the distributor has a sales meeting once a week at 5:00 pm. for one hour. At this sales meeting, sometimes one of their manufacturer's sales reps or sales manager make a presentation of a new product or one they would like the distributor salesmen to promote, and in addition to product knowledge, offer a "spiff" or reward or prize for their sales of this product. Distributor salesmen have a choice of several similar items to sell in almost all categories. Vendor salesmen must try to motivate them to choose their product to sell over all others.

The distributor salesmen have to consider the profit margin on each product they sell, because each salesman is expected to maintain a certain profit margin of, say, at least 40 percent. The salesman has to decide to go for the vendor's prize money or sell the similar house item with no reward except the high profit margin.

I have some experience with distributor salesmen and there are some super salesmen selling their hearts out for their distributor. The same principles of "street smart" selling apply to get to No. 1. There is a big difference in the type of selling, but it's still selling. The distributor salesman must try to earn a very good living for himself and his family within a few square blocks or a couple of square miles with several hundred products. He or she is home every night.

The "outside salesman," on the other hand, covers an entire state or several states with fewer products and is on the road and away from home a lot. Outside salesmen sell higher ticket items and can be a thousand miles or more away from the home office. The outside salesman plans and decides where and when to go. He has much less supervision. It is a completely different selling culture. This book was written from the experience of an outside salesman, primarily for outside salesmen, but this is sound selling advice for anyone who wants to sell and earn to the top of his potential.

2. Manufacturers That Have Chosen To Market Through Distributors

Salesmen for these manufacturers that sell their products through distributors primarily call on their distributors, entertaining and presenting to the distributor salesmen. Sometimes the vendor salesman will make a prospect sales call with the distributor salesman to sell his product and land a new customer and make points with his distributor.

A Sales Manager for this manufacturer may fire a weak distributor and replace him with a bigger and stronger distributor who will have a better chance of selling more for the manufacturer. He will add new distributors where there is no coverage. He will spend most of his time with his major market distributors, some of who are nationwide. This Sales Manager will travel like an outside salesman or even more, and will benefit from this book. No matter how good sales managers think they are, and they are good, they will benefit if they pick up only one new idea or one they've forgotten, by reading this book. Then, they should pass it on to their distributor's salesmen.

22

Coordination Is The Key

1. National Customers

If you sell to a branch plant of a national multi-facility corporation, all requests for a price quotation or quantity discount must be coordinated through your home office. All branch plants in different states must receive the same pricing for similar quantities per order. Your company will lose the national customer if each sales representative quotes different prices or offers discounts on his own.

2. Federal Government

Companies and sales reps should take into consideration the fact that any product sold to the federal government must be, by law, the same as the lowest price that has been offered to anyone for that product.

The Pentagon
Department of Defense photograph by Master Sgt.
Ken Hammond, US Air Force

3. International Sales

In big cities with ocean ports such as Los Angeles, there are multiple container shipments going overseas every day. Companies in Asia are ordering huge quantities of goods and supplies from the United States every day. If your company has hired an international sales manager who travels to Asia, you must coordinate with him, but you should get credit for any sales initiated by you. The international sales person can't possibly cover all of the hundreds or possibly thousands of sales agents all over the United States representing Asian Companies. These agents look for vendors across the U.S. to fill the orders of the overseas companies they represent.

When you locate them, they ask for your very best price, they want freight paid and every break you can give them for the big orders they will give you. There must be a profit between your price and the price they charge their Asian customer. Some U.S. firms will pay freight, but some don't, to a "trans-shipper" in Los Angeles, Long Beach, San Francisco, Oakland or Seattle, who then pack the goods in containers and ship them to Asia.

This is big business. The sales representative who has the shipping point within his territory either gets full credit or splits with the rep that initiated the order. There might be an agent in Houston who orders from the local sales rep, but ships out of the Port of Los Angeles or the Port of Long Beach.

If your company fields an in-house sales force and you manufacture the product the agent's customer specifies, they have to buy from you regardless of price or freight considerations. You get list price, the agent adds freight, his mark-up and that is the price to his customer overseas. If your company sells through distributors in some areas and also has factory sales reps, the agents now can buy your company's specified product from whoever offers the lowest price and best freight terms. The factory sales rep will in most cases lose.

American companies sub-contract work to Asian manufacturers who must comply with parts, chemicals and other products that have been listed in the specifications that must be followed by the Asian companies. Their agents in America must search for and buy the products listed in the specifications. The ports of Los Angeles and Long Beach, which together are the nation's busiest ports, handle *$360 billion per year* in trade. Are you and your company enjoying any of this business? If not, who is? And this is the business of just two ports located in Los Angeles.

23

'War Stories'

1. In Football and In Selling, Blocking The Competition Out And Stopping An 80-Yard (Drum) Return Are Keys To Success

"War Stories" are rare and unusual stories of pride in great sales that have been accomplished by perseverance, cleverness, ingenuity, common sense and salesmanship, as told by the salesman himself or their sales manager.

This first "War Story" is about using common sense to keep competition from discovering your gold mine. One of my airline customers bought 80 drums of aircraft cleaner from me and these 80 drums were lined up against a chain-link fence facing the street. I "suggested" to my contact that he put plastic strapping through the fence links to hide the 80 drums from the street where competitive salesmen roamed like birds of prey. In this way my contact wouldn't be bothered by a swarm of salesmen wasting his valuable time. He complied, and the gold rush and further competition stopped. Nothing is easy! When the airline's Controller, while walking through the area, saw the 80 drums lined up, he was "upset" and told my contact to return the 80 drums. My contact called me in and apologetically said he was told to return the 80 drums because of the large amount of money this big purchase tied up. Our manufacturing plant was just a few miles away.

No way was I going to take back a $32,000 order of airplane cleaner that they were currently using to wash their airplanes. I asked to meet with the Controller (Accountant) and told him that we had paid the freight on the eighty 500-pound drums and that he would have to pay the freight back to the plant. He agreed, but I wasn't finished. I reminded him this was a product they have been using for many years and this was a sale at a discount price. He didn't care, as it was tying up too much money. Now I hit him where it hurts. I informed him that there would be a 25 percent restocking charge, or $8,000, plus freight. No contest.

They kept the 80 drums and my contact was happy we won as he didn't like an accountant second-guessing his order decisions.

2. Yes, This Is Selling Too

Another major charter airline company had a fleet of Boeing jet aircraft and used outside contractors to clean them. I sold 40 drums of aircraft cleaner at a time every six weeks. My eloquent sales presentation went like this. About every five weeks, I would drive the 60 miles to the airport, park and look through the partially covered chain-link fence to count the drums of each of my two cleaners used to clean the planes. If they were not quite ready for another 40 drums, I would go to the reception area, call my contact who looked like "Mr. T" and tell him I had checked the drums and it's just about time for another order, but not this week, so I'll have it shipped next week when you will be ready. "Is that OK?" How eloquent can you get? Rather than coming back again next week and wasting time, wrap up the order now and be on your way. I've got to tell you the complete story if you are going to be "street smart." I occasionally treated my contact to lunch. At Christmas, this business friend is on my list. He is a very good customer who trusts me to order for him. He travels a lot and I know what he drinks, so I give him a fully loaded travel bar and a comparable gift the next year. It is a small "thank you" for all the commissions our good relationship earns.

Now back to the main story with this airline and the cleaning contractor. The airline contracted with the U.S. Government to wash the Boeing 747 in which the President of the United States of America flies all over the world. My company's chemical cleaners are to be used and they asked for my help in getting ready. We had two weeks before the first Boeing 747 would fly in from Omaha to be washed with my chemicals and as it turned out, my equipment. This is called *"service"* over and above the line of duty. I got an agreement from my company to pay for the necessary pressure washers to pump the thickened chemical up hill to the five-story tall tail of the 747. My customer agreed to pay 25¢ a gallon extra until the equipment cost was paid, and then they would own the equipment and the price per gallon would revert back to normal.

We built "wash carts" that held two drums and an air pump to spray a "gel" cleaner onto the aircraft. The gel cleaner would stick to the aircraft and a maintenance worker would agitate it with a soft white rectangular "3M" pad on a long handle from a *"cherry picker"* and then the gel cleaner and soil would be rinsed off with de-ionized water. "D I Water" leaves no residue on drying.

Bob Felgen (R) on a "cherry picker" at United Airlines

When the big day arrived, we were ready with about twenty five men with their equipment and four *"cherry pickers,"* wash carts, drums, pumps and drums of *"gel"* cleaner and plenty of extra cleaner and extra pumps. Previously, I had to get clearance from the government to be there at the time of the cleaning process and had two or three badges around my neck. I would have given almost anything to have a camera or a professional photographer take pictures of me and forty drums of my company's product in front of the "United States of America, "Air Force One," Boeing 747 President's official airplane. *Not!* Cameras were not allowed and this was enforced by Marines surrounding the airplane and us, each of whom had their automatic weapons at the ready. Oh, how I would have liked the President of my company, *Mr. Louis Brunner*, to see this. No one from my company was there to see this *great moment in "selling!"* No one would believe this!

Air Force One
U.S. Air Force photo by Airman 1ˢᵗ Class Jason P. Robertson

At 6:00 am, right on time, here it came through the fog, taxiing to the exact spot we had designated as the wash rack area. There was no hangar and we were out in the open. We had trained the workers on how to proceed with the cleaning. Wheel wells, flap wells, landing gear teams went right to work. The wash crews on *"cherry pickers"* started at the top of the tail and completed agitating a section, and then it was rinsed before the soil held in suspension could dry down. Walls are cleaned from the bottom up, to avoid streaking. Common sense and experience with aircraft cleaning requires an airplane to be cleaned from the top down. U.S. Air Force Inspectors watched the process, as the contractor would not be paid if there had been any damage to the aircraft or was not cleaned properly. The contractor's foremen and I supervised the process, which went smoothly and efficiently and was "accepted" by the U.S. Air Force Inspector.

This took the whole day's prime selling time but I wouldn't trade this experience for ten average prospect/customer calls, and consider the creditability gained with my very big and important customer. What do you think this big account will say to all the other salesmen who will knock on their door selling aircraft cleaners? *There is much more to selling and holding customers than most companies, sales books and consultants know.* It helps to be *"street smart."*

3. The 'Philadelphia Story'

As Asst. Natl. Sales Manager, I flew into Philadelphia to meet with our salesman to find out why our chemical company was not getting any of the 100 drum concrete seal business a major national chain bought every year to re-coat their huge regional office complex and distribution center. We were one of only three approved vendors. The other two divided this huge dollar business between them and we got not even one drum, let alone a third.

Our salesman, who was struggling in general, didn't know why we weren't getting any of the business because he had called on them from time to time and he said he got along well with the maintenance foreman, who was in charge of buying the 100 drums of concrete seal, worth about $55,000.

I knew our approved concrete seal was as good, or better, than the other two manufacturer's sealers. Our concrete seal was being used in the other regions of this national chain with great satisfaction, so why weren't we getting any or all of this business?

I was led through three levels of catacombs to a small office and maintenance room that is far removed from the executive suites and there I met an unpretentious man who stood up and shook our hands. I asked him, as an approved vendor, why we were not getting any of his seal business? He answered: *"Your man doesn't see me at Christmas!"* Our salesman apologized and said he would come to see him this Christmas.

As soon as we got outside I asked our "sales representative", not to be compared with a "salesman," if he understood what this man was really telling us! He answered: "I don't give gifts to get business!" Well, what ever you are doing isn't working! (Our company did not condone gift giving like some of the other chemical companies.) (Some chemical company's even require their salesmen to order a specified dollar amount of giveaways, which is then deducted from their commission.) Almost all large companies send letters to their vendors telling them it is against their policy for their employees to accept gifts. (Our salesmen were paid straight commission with a "draw" and paid all of their own expenses.)

Some will disagree with my view on how the above situation should be handled, but the solution is easy if you are a professional salesman with the desire to be "number one" in sales and income to provide more than just food and shelter for yourself and your family.

I tried to explain to our sales representative that for a $25 bottle of liquor or a two pound box of candy, or a Butterball Turkey before Christmas with a nice Christmas card saying: "Thank you for the time and courtesy you showed me this year." "Merry Christmas to you and your family," you can probably have at least one third of the seal business this coming year. The total amounts to $55,000 and our one third equals $18,333 at approximately 15 percent or $2,750, in commission for a $25.00 *"thank you"* gift at Christmas. You or anyone would gladly give me $25.00 if I then gave you or them $2,750 cash in a trade! This is what I want you to do; *"trade"* $ 25.00 for $2,750 that will now benefit your family instead of your competitor's family. Just do it!!! Hell, you can afford to give him a case with that kind of return on your money! Don't wait for Christmas! Invite him and his wife to dinner at a fine Philadelphia restaurant, and it is tax deductible!

HE DIDN'T DO IT! This man qualifies for the chicken of the year award, the letter of the law award and the accountant of the year award, because he's not a salesman. This man is a sheep in salesman's clothing! Professional Salesmen *create* and take advantage of all opportunities to increase sales and their income, in their *burning desire* to strive to be "number one." They let no opportunity slip by, especially on purpose. This wasn't the only situation with this representative and I made the decision to replace him. I then hired one of the other two salesmen who knew how to say "thank you" and who as a result were getting all of the seal business; "Merry Christmas!"

4. IT Pays To Cover All The Bases

U.S. Navy Procurement Offices were located in Oakland, CA, next to the Alameda Naval Air Station and Naval Base. Because of my business with the aircraft carriers, I had made a call there and left my cards. Procurement didn't make the decision on which flight deck cleaner each aircraft carrier used, they only processed the Air Department Officer's request. They did make decisions on thousands of other items for U.S. Navy ships that all used other chemical products. I told them that my company's flight deck cleaner had been chosen by the three Aircraft Carriers home based in Alameda and if I could be of any help with any other chemical products they used, we could offer immediate delivery as our manufacturing plant was located in Richmond, CA next door to Oakland and Alameda. I met several buyers and they all had my card when I left.

Several weeks later I took my week off to visit with my Mother, Lenore, in Oakbrook, IL, a suburb of Chicago. While sitting at my Mother's kitchen table eating breakfast, the phone rang and it was a girl from my office who told me the Navy had called and wanted me to quote a price on fifty drums of flight deck cleaner today. This was for the USS Midway permanently home-based in Japan. I called procurement back within a few minutes, quoted the price and he gave me the order. Having earned over $2,500 commission while on vacation, eating breakfast two thousand three hundred miles away from my territory in about twenty minutes was amazing, even to me. It pays to *cover all bases* all over your territory. Some would call it luck. I call it hard work, experience and making your presence known all over your territory by planting seeds that germinate into extra orders that can propel you to the *top in sales and money earned.*

24

Bloopers

1. Little Things Mean A Lot

I'm confessing these major *"bloopers"* with the hope other salesmen will learn some of the missteps that can happen inadvertently and unintentionally and where big dollars are at stake and lost for lack of this kind of experience. These are lessons carved deeply into my memory so I won't ever make the same mistakes again and am telling you so that you won't make the same mistakes that I made.

I pulled up in front of "Bargain Town U.S.A." in Chicago in my station wagon full of tricycles and fire engine pedal toys. Bargain Town U.S.A. was a giant multi-store chain of toy stores and a very important prospective buyer of boxcar loads of bulk toys. I was rather new to selling bulk toys, but it was a good brand and I thought it would be fun to sell toys. I had recently gotten back from seeing and selling the new line at the New York Market "Toy Fair." I had just received and assembled my tricycles and pedal cars and fire engine and was anxious to get going and show and sell these beautiful and well-built new "bulk toys," as they were called.

I called "Bargain Town U.S.A." and made an appointment to come in and show the new line to the principals. This was my biggest potential prospect by far and I was anxious to start off big and was excited about showing this great new line to this huge toy chain.

I was told to bring my samples in and set them up and the principals would come down in a few minutes. I was parked outside at the curb near the front door, but it was no simple task to bring in all those tricycles and pedal cars and line them up according to price. Finally, the owners came down and I introduced myself and started talking about the top-of-the-line beautiful metallic gold tricycle trimmed in red racing stripes. It was beautiful, but before I finished talking, one of the owners was looking at the gold tricycle and the wheel "squeaked" and he kicked the tricycle hard and said, "This meeting is over! If you don't think enough about your samples to oil them and simonize them before you show your line, we don't think enough about the line to buy it." He then walked away with the others. The presentation was over. I felt terrible and packed up and went home and oiled all the toys and bought some Simonize and simonized them all. It was too late for my hope of selling carloads this year and they would have me at a disadvantage in future price negotiations, if any. They don't call it "Bargain Town" for nothing.

First, I should have practiced at smaller customers and prospects before tackling the big one. The smaller stores probably wouldn't have said anything about the squeak or, hopefully, they would mention it or I would have oiled it before the "big presentation." I probably wouldn't have thought to simonize them as I thought they looked good as is. The rude, but correct, man at Bargain Town was right as they did look much better "simonized." He taught me a hard lesson I have never forgotten and I am sure it was the reason I always checked my samples, to this day, with "buyer's eyes," to make sure they were perfect. So, practice and iron-out any bugs at your smaller customers before you present to the majors and make sure your samples sell themselves.

2. Flip Chart or Wal-Mart

In this next "blooper" situation, I was Vice President of National Accounts for a company that manufactured floor finish and was a prime supplier to most of the national chain stores. I had been able to get an appointment to make a presentation to Wal-Mart in their Bentonville, AR headquarters along with our salesman from Little Rock. I knew what we had to offer by heart and knew what was important to Wal-Mart, *price*! We were up against Johnson's Wax who I knew were higher priced and we had 165 excellent hands-on professional sales/service reps and four Regional Managers covering the United States. Johnson had some well-trained company salesmen, but mostly sold through "distributors" whose salesmen in general were not well trained or consistent in their knowledge of "floor care." We surveyed every store for all our customers every quarter as to safety condition of the floors as it pertains to "slip and fall" and had never lost a lawsuit for our customers in the event of someone falling and filing suit because of these "safe floor" reports and safe floors. We had a very good shot of landing, at the least, a few "test stores" from this meeting and then earn the right to supply one district and so on until we supplied the entire chain's stores nationwide.

My company was family owned but had recently been acquired in a "hostile takeover." I had new bosses who were recently graduated from a famous M.B.A. University. They had someone draw a sales presentation "flip-chart" for the company and insisted, over my objections, that I use it for my Wal-Mart presentation.

It told, with artist's rendering, of our three manufacturing plants, about the founder of the company, etc. It was a formidable and heavy "flip-chart" that was a painful presentation for me to give and the buyers to tolerate. After 14 minutes, they all had turned into "skeletons" from boredom. It formally and completely missed the bull's eye. It told of whom we are and not what Wal-Mart wanted to hear, how much money we would save them!

All of a sudden, the "buyer" stood up and said, "Thank you for the presentation. We only allow 15 minutes for each presentation," and left the cubical. We tried to stop them by telling them we hadn't finished, but they wanted to see and hear no more! This was worse than my first sales call! I learned another lesson, but an expensive one. I wondered how many hard lessons we have to endure before we die. When dealing with people, I'm afraid the lessons will never end. But, lessons learned is money earned and professional salesmen never give up and keep right on selling, hopefully improving.

I am sure that, if we could have talked person to person without "canned" props and told them of the benefits, value and pricing structure we offer to national chains, we would have been granted more time. Again, the first time with a new and foreign presentation that some non-street smart person created should *never* be presented the first time to the *"mother of all majors!"* I should have told them no, but I was torn between trying to cooperate with the new owners and doing what was our only hope of selling this huge chain store. I chose wrong. In hindsight, the owners would have forgotten their anger at my refusal to use their school-like chart if I had come home "with the bacon!" It never dawned on me until agonizing thoughts later, that I should have agreed to use the school boy flip chart, left it in the car, and given a bulls-eye to the target "street smart" "big money" presentation of benefits to them. End.

Everyone will think I'm like "Mr. Magoo" with the black cloud over my head if I tell of any more screw-ups, so I'll tell just one more.

3. 'Anything That Can Go Wrong, Will'

I lived in Mill Valley just north of the Golden Gate Bridge and, as Western Regional Sales Manager, flew to Los Angeles from San Francisco often. I had made an appointment to meet with the person in charge of buying my product category for a very big supermarket chain with regional headquarters in Los Angeles. The buyer told me to fly into the Orange County (John Wayne) Airport as it was closer to their offices than LAX. I had never flown into Orange County or ever been to this regional office.

I had arranged for an early flight as my appointment was at 10:00 am. My flight arrived late into Orange County and I hurried to the rental car area of the old airport, which had only one rental car agency with at least ten people waiting to rent a car. I was in trouble! I asked someone to save my place in line (no cell phones yet) while I called my contact at the supermarket office to tell him of the situation at the airport and that I most probably would be running late.

I was floored and taken totally by surprise by his reply! He said: *"you blew it"!* I have other appointments lined up all day and won't be able to see you." The plane was late and the long line at the car rental excuse was true, but didn't fly! He only had set aside so much time for our appointment and, if missed or was late, there was no more time available. I was surprised at his harsh reaction as we had a very nice conversation in setting up the appointment and he was helpful in the airport selection, although I might have been better served at LAX with which I was familiar and had multiple car rental agencies.

I managed to salvage a meeting with the Director of Maintenance for the Southern California stores, but nothing ever came of it. The original contact didn't answer my subsequent calls and the opportunity was gone. This was entirely my fault. I shouldn't have cut it so close flying into a strange airport and driving to a facility to which I had never been. And, to make it worse, the buyer didn't know me and I didn't know him. To him I was just another sloppy, inefficient salesman that now he didn't have to see. The opportunity was granted, and lost.

My mistake was that I didn't fly in the night before, which was a Sunday. The lesson of all this is you should always plan to fly in the night before any important morning meeting. If it's not possible to fly on Sunday night, the appointment should be "steered" to Tuesday or the rest of the week.

Fortunately, the successes far outnumber the mistakes and, like great baseball players who make occasional errors and fail two of every three times at bat, they are still considered "stars" and earn millions of dollars. It is much better if we can see the mistakes of others, learn from their experience and move on. It would be better if our occasional mistakes happened at very small accounts. Mistakes, errors and misjudgments at major prospects or customers can, and most of the time does, have a serious negative effect on what is intended to be accomplished. A salesman never forgets a big mistake and always wonders *what might have been.*

The Wal-Mart story, above, if sold, eventually would have been worth well over $5,000,000 every year. The presentation prop from the "classroom" probably cost about $500 to $1,000, but it really cost a very probable $5,000,000 annually because the presentation was not *street smart!"*

I had written about my "Bloopers" with some trepidation before this issue of BusinessWeek arrived in my mail. I went ahead with it to help other salesmen and sales managers learn from my mistakes and this BusinessWeek cover and article validates my decision.

In the July 10, 2006 issue of BusinessWeek magazine, the cover reads: "Eureka We Failed! How Smart Companies Learn From Their Flops." By: Jena McGregor. Also appearing on the cover is an article entitled "Plus: My Favorite Mistake (featuring) Jeff Immelt of GE, Neville Isdell of Coke, Helen Greiner of iRobot and Pete Carroll of USC."

On page 42 of this issue of BusinessWeek, the headline reads: "How Failure Breeds Success. Everyone fears failure. But breakthroughs depend on it. The best companies embrace their mistakes and learn from them." By: Jena McGregor.

25

Master Salesmen's Secrets To Success

The following are "War Stories" and secrets on selling techniques from some of the "Master Salesmen." The references to "Brulin" in these stories, is the specialty chemical manufacturer these "Master Salesmen" represented and whose selling success stories apply equally well to other industry's products. These stories are about people skills and desire more than about the products, but the products must work or nothing else will. Enjoy and learn from these "War Stories" by the "Master Salesmen."

1. Ralph Sauder, Master Salesman, Illinois

"I've lived in exile now for 16 years, sometimes known as retirement, but I remember the good old Brulin Company days like it was yesterday.

I always told my customers, new and old, that I've been with Brulin X amount of years and I'll be the same person calling on you next month and next year. I always wanted to be known for my best qualities: I am always *reliable and dependable*". I think that's what everybody wants.

I'm also a *now* person. Any question about a shipment or any question about a product will be taken care of *now*. I'd get on their phone and call our 800 number and have an answer while I'm there. Many times I called our chief chemist and had him talk to the customer *now*.

I was very successful with Caterpillar, Inc., supplying all the plants in Illinois and Iowa. They never knew that I had eighty drums of 815MX, bar coded and labeled with Bldg. Y 49 (their warehouse) ready to go. I loved saying: "The shipment will be in building Y 49 first thing in the morning." It was an overnight, leaving Indy at 5:00 pm.

I always wore a white shirt and tie, with a suit or sport coat. "If you're going to talk business, look like a business man." I was always a man of my word.

Bob, I could go on and on about war stories as I'm sure all the other salesmen can. I loved what I did and I loved making money. Best wishes on your new book."

2. Hoytt Childress, Master Salesman, Miami

"It was most surprising, that the head maintenance engineer for all stores of a very big national retail chain, who was responsible for selecting one of the approved vendors for each new store, was to say the least, a "difficult buyer". We were not getting our fair share of new store business. He would not talk to me, wouldn't have a meal with me and I couldn't do anything for him.

After one frustratingly short sales call I asked: "why don't you stop by the hotel and have a drink?" He said OK. After two drinks I said: "Let's have a bite of dinner." He said OK. He mentioned a certain kind of drink and we drank several. I never discussed business over a drink. After that evening, we received more than our fair share of new store assignments and we were now working well together, not as strangers, but as friends with something in common.

When "canvassing," I always carried two items in my bag, two different types of product to demonstrate. Always take in something different to a current customer. Always be ready to make a demonstration.

At the end of the day when you are ready to go home, make one more canvass call. This equals extra sales.

Call on the people that do the work. Don't make a presentation to the "buyer." Go to the department head. Go in the back door or gate and start asking questions.

A major national chain store was using my biggest competitor's products and he was in solid. I got in one small item. One day I was in the store and met the competitor's rep, who was with the store manager. I suggested that we each ship in one drum of product, *no charge*, and see which product best gave the manager what he wanted. The manager agreed, but the competitor wouldn't do that. He had nothing to gain and everything to lose. I had nothing to lose and everything to gain. I shipped in a free drum of material anyway.

55-gallon drum

They liked it and the fact that I, and my company, gave a free drum worth over $500.00 to prove our superiority and his vendor wouldn't, made the difference. As a result, we enjoyed this customer's repeat business for many years. Would you invest $500.00 to earn many, many times that much for the next twenty years? I enjoyed selling!"

3. Leo Ray, Master Salesman, Seattle

"My Brulin Co. sales career paled compared to before mentioned men, but I did enjoy developing new accounts, cold calls, etc. One method I used with success was this: On first contact with a potential account, I introduced the company and products that would be of benefit, etc. If a demonstration was not possible on the first call, a time and place was selected and I would ask permission to write my name and time of "demo" on the prospect's calendar (supplied by a competitor) hanging on the wall by his desk. The prospect then had the pleasure of seeing my name every day until I returned. What this normally established was that I was organized, dependable and confident in the quality of the products, which spoke for themselves.

Bob, your letter revived memories of a great company, great salesmen, great relationships and I know your book will become a "must read training manual" for other comparable sales companies. Thanks for the opportunity to express my feeling, ironically on Memorial Day Weekend."

4. Jeff Cornes, Master Salesman, Tampa, Florida

"Master Salesman" Jeff Cornes sent me this "War Story" on what is involved in selling a major supermarket chain maintenance supplies, mainly floor care products, and other selling tips to be of help to current and future salesmen to sell and maintain "the big ones."

"If you are going to take on an account that is two to three times what most people sell, you need to be prepared to do some hard work and learn more than you ever needed before. Also remember what you get, you are going to lose. You are going to make some powerful friends and allies and also some powerful competitors. Your biggest competition may be your own company trying to make above-average profit and becoming greedy and making your efforts a "house account." (Author's comment: This never happened with The Brulin Company.)

The joys of victory when you are told you're the one, "you're selected," and that you are going to earn $75,000 plus on that one account for the year will make you ecstatic.

For a grocery chain of 100+ stores averaging more than 40,000 square feet, you will probably test three, four or five stores of varying traffic, age, location and sales volume. The test is a complete strip (stripping off the old dirty floor finish) and wax (two coats of floor finish) of all test stores, monitoring all costs to the square foot and then maintaining the floors and re-strip as necessary. The floor care program must be easy for new and unskilled maintenance workers.

The management of the floor program must be run by the number two man in the store. The manager is too busy, and number three and four do not have enough power to control.

Strip jobs done twice annually work well to achieve cleanliness and stay within budget. We created a professional video, with test, for training. We put on one district at a time, kicked off with a district meeting of Vice President, District Manager, Store Manager and the "number two" man. Floor appearance is within the top three reasons with price and selection for the reason a supermarket is chosen by a shopper.

The sales rep. has to be a friend to the store and have the demeanor of its top management. With all those people and stores, there will be some failures and tough problems. The account will try to own you and your time. They will ask for price roll-backs and they will bring in competition with test stores. Rollbacks are based on the supermarket chain giving you increased business and factoring in the raw materials discounts given to the manufacturer for the increased volume of raw materials purchased. The District Managers love to have nice lunches and often sports golf and other tickets are greatly appreciated. VP's were taken to expensive dinners with their wives from time to time. I purposely minimized visits from my home office. I would do this and other large accounts again.

I would recommend, after establishing a great base of income, huge, giant accounts be pursued with great vigor. You will develop extraordinary skills and power. The personal rewards can be enormous in friendships and growth. By the way, my big supermarket account was approached through the safety, insurance and real estate department. Next was a presentation to the VP and Senior VP. The CEO observed and gave his approval. Purchasing was *told* by the Senior Vice President after the testing was complete, to bring truck loads of product into the warehouse. First year's business was $500,000. Discounted prices resulted in 40 tractor trailer loads in a year. Maintenance was a $5 million dollar cost with chemicals and labor and the third highest expense for the grocery chain.

Their sister company manufactured specialty chemicals and *was* their supplier. We provided a higher appearance, more cost effective, easier program and "expert witness testimony" for "slip and fall" litigations.

Sales tip: Either do everything, selling many types of chemicals to a diverse group of customers, or *specialize*! I learned six chemicals extremely well: Stripper, Non-Slip Floor Finish, Seal, Neutral Cleaner, Cleaner and Restorer. Then I focused on floor care, then chains of stores. Then I focused on larger chains of stores and then huge chains of stores. Not hospitals, not aircraft, no "Joe's Garage" and not industry. I only went after retail chains and grocery store chains with the six floor-care products.

Know your buyers and make them your wonderful friends. Be the most dependable, most reliable, your word is your bond person. If you promise the goods to be there, make sure they are there, every time. Be available with cell phone, e-mails, faxes, and a secretary. Sleep with your cell phone on, beside you. Your competition does! The more and bigger accounts you sell, the more you're a target. If your competition gives a five gallon pail free for a test at a valuable account, you give a 55 gallon drum! If your competition takes a man in and does a test, you take five men in and do a huge test! If your competition gives pretty wall charts that are 3 x 4 feet, make your wall chart, with the maintenance proce-dures, 8 x 12 feet! *If you're the "Big Dog," act like the "Big Dog!"*

Very well stocked customers are harder for your competition to sell! At $60,000 commission per chain, hire a secretary to call customers for mundane reorders and, keeping in touch, with the customer's permission. Make up reorder sheets to be faxed or called in to your secretary/assistant.

In large malls, take the maintenance managers from competing stores (Sears, J.C. Penney, etc.) to lunch at the same time and leave the table so they can talk about you. Do the same for the operations managers. Remember, you are *first* in the people business, *first* in store appearance, *first* in production and *first* in cost reduction."

5. Hank Bonsall, Master Salesman, San Francisco

"I was once asked to put a test strip down at a hanger at the Oakland Airport. I knew my competition was a seasoned (and clever) Brulin salesman so the first call I made was to the P.A. (purchasing agent) and requested my test be postponed a few days. My hope was that this Brulin guy would "show his hand" and I would be able to upstage his test.

I arrived at the hangar and the P.A. gave me the area my test was to be placed. He felt it unfair to tell me where the Brulin test was and I reluctantly agreed (under my breath I uttered an: oh sh—). I told him I had to go out to the car and get the cleaner, etch and concrete seal. Being the seasoned guy I was, I headed for the dumpster to see what this Brulin guy had used and, lo and behold, there was an empty Brulin can of concrete seal!! It was one of Brulin's most expensive seals. I could hardly restrain my cleverness.

I completed my test and left confident I had done him in. I called the P.A. a day or two later only to find my price was by far the highest. I was crushed. How did he do it? Well what this guy did was suggest and test a low priced chlorinated rubber seal and "plant" an empty gallon can of the very expensive moisture cure polyurethane seal in the dumpster. I had been outsmarted! I still admire this guy. As a matter of fact he was once my boss and was instrumental in my joining The Brulin Company. We remain good friends. Oh yes, his name is Felgen. We have shared many laughs over the years and I can *never* remember having my pants off so successfully by a competitor.

My second tale relates to the *Moscone Center* in San Francisco. We were asked to bid on sealing the convention floor of this new building. I went to see the floor and there were cement trucks parked around the block. The building was behind schedule. I looked at the floor and you could see small eruptions of water due to the "green" cement and the fact that the floor was below sea level. I spoke to the facilities manager and he told me the specs were for a high solids urethane to be applied. I told him that was not the appropriate product. He asked me where I got my degree in architecture. I tried to tell him I was only trying to save him some grief. He didn't understand (he was from the South East, Tennessee I Think) that in the "Bay Area," moisture under pressure from below ground forces its way up and pops and peels back any concrete paint or seal that doesn't "breathe." The high-solids sealer that was "specked in" didn't breathe and was forced to peel up. I turned down the bid, but told him I was open to doing it right when the floor went bad. I must admit I said that with a smile and the conversation ended up on a friendly note. What was needed was a low solids chlorinated rubber seal that "breathes" and won't pop.

I guess it was four of five months later when Bill, the Facilities Manager, called and asked me to come over and look at the floor. It was a mess. I can't remember the number of drums of D370PV seal stripper we used to get the popped and pealing urethane seal off, or the number of drums of a penetrating seal called Clear Cement Seal Coat we used with a topping of Century Floor Finish, but it got Bob Felgen's attention. This re-do was a yearly deal for the next three years until Bill left Moscone. I think that was the largest single order I ever wrote for The Brulin Company. I took three days (day and night) to complete the job.

If my limited memory can recall any other tales I will forward them to you. All else is good and I hope the same is the case with you. My best to Ann and my fondest regards to you."

6. Bob Felgen, Master Salesman, Northern and Southern, California

"The USS Enterprise Nuclear Aircraft Carrier had finished testing many flight deck cleaners and didn't allow any salesmen, who were mostly women, to take part in the tests. We had sold flight deck cleaner to the USS Coral Sea and it worked perfectly for them. We had met the USS Enterprise Air Officer in charge of flight deck cleaning, but he relied on a sailor of lowest rank who drove the riding scrubber vehicle (Please see picture of riding scrubber in chapter thirteen, number five, after seventh paragraph) to tell him which cleaner he thought did the best job. We are talking close to $100,000 worth of flight deck cleaner. The sailor, "expert in cleaning" that he was, chose a cleaner from a major competitor and when I came on board after the test was completed, there were 30 drums of this arch-competitors cleaner already on the flight deck.

I was told by the officer in charge not to feel too bad as the sailor marked my sample with "NO GOOD" and all the other losers with: "not worth a sh__!" That's the same feeling one gets as your girl friend tells you you're a wonderful person and I will always love you very much, but I'm going to marry the other guy. I was crushed! I know my flight deck/ hangar deck cleaner worked very well on the USS Coral Sea and I couldn't accept a "*no good*" rating from a scrubber driver who probably couldn't care less which cleaner was used. *Unless*, the competitive salesman got to him somehow even with a "motivational" phone call. I'm not saying it's what happened, but men have been killed for a lot less than $100,000.

Tied up at the adjoining dock, for a re-fit was the USS Coral Sea just back from a six-month tour of duty. I went on board and to the familiar "Air Department" where I knew the officers who had bought and used my flight deck cleaner on their recent tour of duty, which was completed "without incident." This means the flight deck was squeaky clean and no aircraft or flight deck equipment had slid off the deck and into the ocean in rough seas. If there is an *"incident,"* the air officer in charge of flight deck safety and cleanliness can never be promoted, even if he is off duty and was asleep in his bunk at the time!

I told the story of the test and the decision of the USS Enterprise Air Officer to take the word of an indifferent sailor who rated the product they had used successfully, *"no good."* My USS Coral Sea customers, who had become friends before they sailed six months ago, told me to invite the USS Enterprise Air Department Commander to a lunch at the "Whale's Tail Restaurant" near the navy base and they would *"sell"* him on using my flight deck cleaner that had worked so well for them. It was a long shot as the competitive product was already on deck, but it was a "last of the 9th with two strikes opportunity." Actually, it was really a protest after the game was lost situation, but for the cost of a lunch, I had nothing to lose and everything to gain.

The five USS Coral Sea Officers ordered a couple of drinks before the commander from the USS Enterprise arrived and the mood was boisterous after six months at sea with no alcoholic drinks allowed. I glanced at the door and there he was spit and polish in his white officer's uniform and he looked like Robert Redford. I introduced everyone and the waitress asked what he would like to drink and when he ordered a "Diet Tab," I knew I was finished!

However, after the USS Coral Sea Officers told him he was crazy to use an untested cleaner when he could assure his promotion by using a flight deck cleaner that has been proven to work perfectly on an actual six month cruise. He agreed to another test between the winner of the first test and my proven cleaner that was used successfully on the USS Coral Sea.

The "Scrub-off" was observed by the ship's Captain and Officers, which included all of the Air Department Officers. I was allowed on deck for the test and to my surprise the Air Department Commander told the Captain: "Mr. Felgen will supervise the mixing of the chemical in the scrubbers." The two large riding scrubbers were about thirty yards away from the crowd of officers and they assigned a sailor to help with the mixing of the chemicals into "soap tanks" on each scrubber. My competitor was not invited to participate in the test. The

Commander walked with me part of the way toward the scrubbers and told me, "You had better win!" What would you do? I was in charge of adding the competitor's chemical as well as mine to a measured amount of water in each scrubbers "soap tank."

Photo of USS Enterprise courtesy of U.S. Navy footage/video

The two big riding scrubbers each drove a measured distance on the non-skid flight deck and then back over the same swath, dripping diluted cleaner through stiff rotary scrub brushes to emulsify the grease and oil, scrub it and vacuum it up, in one double pass. The competitive cleaner, with thirty drums on the flight deck near us, didn't touch the grease and their swath looked like the rest of the un-scrubbed deck. My swath was squeaky clean and the light gray color of a newly coated flight deck. Thank you, "Air Officers" of the USS Coral Sea!

The Captain asked the Commander of the Air Department which was the test strip of the 30 drums he pointed to on the flight deck? The Commander pointed to the still dirty test strip. The Captain ordered the competitor's 30 drums to be returned to the manufacturer and an order placed for the other cleaner that worked. My order was for 10,000 gallons of flight deck/hangar deck cleaner. My commission was approximately $1.00 per gallon. That lunch cost about $150.00. There is much more to selling than "Features and Benefits!"

A few days before I closed the USS Enterprise order FOR 10,000 GALLONS, my company had put the West Coast factory workers on "short hours" which meant less pay. Some of the long-time workers would have to look for work elsewhere to support themselves and their families. When this huge order was received at the plant, all workers were called back to "full time" and never went back to short hours and pay ever again. Remember your success helps everyone and *"Nothing happens until somebody sells something!"*

To keep this big sale in perspective, the commission on this sale, while big, is only about one-tenth of the commissions needed to cover expenses, live a comfortable life and save and invest for the future. The other $90,000 or so is earned, not by nine other, "once in a lifetime" sales, but by the hundreds of small and medium size steady repeat-business customers and a *continuous stream of new accounts.* Ninety percent of a salesmen's income is from the day-to-day consistent hard work with the "Bread and Butter" type accounts that provide a base of steady income that enables a salesman to spend the extra time necessary to land and hold the *"big ones!"*

Our thanks go to all the above "Master Salesmen" for sharing their stories and the *"street smart secrets"* of their success, with the hope that you will benefit from them.

"Master Salesman" are always working and continually thinking of how to sell more, sell smarter, sell bigger and beat their competitors. It's sort of like panning for gold. If you slow down or stop, everyone else will pan your gold. "Master Salesmen" do not know they are "Master Salesmen." They make mistakes too and don't sell everybody, but they keep going, keep worrying, keep learning, keep on doing their best with confidence and when the final figures come in, they are *"number one,"* and they are surprised!

Selling is not easy and the purpose of this book is to tell all salesmen, new and experienced, the secrets of successful selling, as told by those of us who have found a way to be successful consistently over time. To the salesmen who have read this book, we hope you have learned some secret strategies that will enable you to become more successful earn a lot of money and hopefully become "Master Salesmen" and enjoy all the benefits you will deserve."

26

The Secrets Of How To Be The 'Best Salesman' And Find Gold

To be the *Best Salesman*, you must have a *burning desire* to be the *Best Salesman*. (If you don't have a *burning desire*, can't think of all the reasons and benefits of being the *Best Salesman* and if you can't believe you can be the *best*, or don't want to do the necessary work, then you better start looking for another profession!)

- To be the *Best Salesman*, you must *work harder* and *smarter* than everyone else.

- To be the *Best Salesman*, you must radiate *confidence*! All the business in your territory belongs to you! I have the greatest and by far the *best product* of everyone else!

- To be the *Best Salesman*, you must *have no fear*! You will not hesitate to call on anyone and are not afraid, but eager, to talk to *the president*!

- To be the *Best Salesman*, you must be *fiercely competitive*! A salesman has to be determined to *beat everyone* in his corporation and in addition put all of his or her competitors *completely out of business*!

- To be the *Best Salesman*, you must *know more about your product line* than everyone else!

- To be the *Best Salesman*, you must know more about your *pricing* and *discount policy* than everyone else!

- To be the *Best Salesman*, you must spend more time *thinking* and *planning* than everyone else!

- To be the *Best Salesman*, you must *find and spend more hours, days and months of selling* than everyone else!

- To be the *Best Salesman*, you must utilize your *sales management* more than everyone else!

- To be the *Best Salesman*, you must be *better at researching and understanding your prospect's needs and wants* more than everyone else!

- To be the Best Salesman, you must be better *organized* than everyone else!

- To be the Best Salesman, you must *manage and prioritize your time* better than everyone else!

- To be the *Best Salesman*, you must be more *consistent* and *persistent* than everyone else!

- To be the *Best Salesman* you must keep your *financial* house in order!

- To be the *Best Salesman*, you must be more *enthusiastic* than everyone else!

- To be the *Best Salesman*, also be the best *husband and father or wife and mother* to your family than everyone else!

- To be the *Best Salesman*, you must always, *every day, make more prospect presentations* than customer sales calls!

- To be the *Best Salesman*, you must *always* maintain *a positive attitude*!

- To be the *Best Salesman, always ask for and get the order*!

Finally, to be the *Best Salesman*, in addition to self-respect, the respect of your bosses and your family, to be the *Best Salesman, "shows you the money!"* (And you will have *earned* every penny of it!)

"What Secrets?"

You have now finished the book and some of you may be muttering to yourselves: *"what secrets?"*

Some of you took notes on the ideas and stories in every chapter of the book that you could use to your advantage in selling more and earning a lot more money. Most didn't. During 47 years of selling, I have observed the methods that consistently work and do not work. In this book I give you the *"secrets"* that work, not just for me, but also for the salesmen I had the responsibility and privilege of managing.

One of the biggest *"secrets"* I learned is that to be *"number one"* in *sales and income* it takes down and dirty *hard work* in the trenches and the *burning desire* to be *"number one."* There is no easy paved highway to get to number one! You may have the *"burning desire"* to be number one but lack the know-how. The know-how is the *"secret"* of the book: "Selling Secrets That Show *You* The Money!"

If you have to ask: "what secrets?" Please read this book again and *take notes* on the *ideas* this book gives you. If you really want to go through all the effort it takes to get to *"number one"* and the *"big money,"* you will get there. The answers are all in this book, but *you* have to do the heavy lifting! This book tells you how, but you have to answer *why* it is worth the effort? Having a *goal* in life is the key. Your future will be better if you have money and worse if you don't! I wish you *GREAT SELLING* and a *GREAT FUTURE!*

Epilogue

Hopefully this salesman's book, "Selling Secrets That Show You The Money," will give every salesman the *street smart* know how to reach the top of his or her sales profession with *vastly increased sales and income.*

I can't give you the desire or the motivation to get you to the top in your corporation, but I can give you the *"know how."* Each salesman has to decide for himself if he or she is willing to make the *adjustments and sacrifices that are necessary* to sell his or her way to the very top.

Desire and Motivation are personal. Some have the desire, but are not willing to do the necessary work. Pride, money or *competitive spirit* is motivation enough for some salesmen to go all-out and overcome all obstacles. Other salesmen, for reasons of their own, have the *"burning desire"* necessary to motivate themselves to the top of their corporate sales force.

In this book, I give salesmen different keys in the road map to No. 1, the big money and also the "minefields" a salesman must successfully navigate to make it to the top. All the selling information in this book won't do any good if you are not willing to do the work. If you supply the desire and your own motivation, this book does offer the *"Street Smart Secrets"* to selling excellence and *financial independence.* You already have the desire or you wouldn't be reading this book. I admire you for reading and trying to become more successful than you already are. Your *positive attitude* and *willingness to learn* will carry you far in your professional selling career. *I wish you Great Selling, Financial Success and Happiness.* Sincerely,

Robert H. Felgen, Master Salesman

References

There are no reference credits in the back of this book because I didn't use any references of other people's ideas to write this book. All of the ideas to help other salesmen come from my personal selling and sales management experiences through the years. This book is short and simple and about the salesman's *attitude* toward his job, his *desire level, competitiveness, work ethic, character and willingness to put in the time and sacrifice necessary to succeed.* I have already crossed the "minefields" in selling for you, and this book maps out the safest route through them *and, even more importantly, how **you** can achieve the selling excellence that leads to the money.*

By the way, I never took a chemistry course in High School or College! What I learned about chemicals was from the company's chemists and my chemical selling ability came from past "street smart" selling experience. *You don't have to major in chemistry to sell chemicals; you have to be a "SALESMAN!"*

Glossary of Sales Terms

A

Ad mats

A fiber impression of a picture and copy, mimicking an ad as it appears in a national magazine, to be used in a customer's local newspaper and coordinated with the vendor's National ads.

Attrition

Attrition is a loss of customers not through any fault of the salesman.

Aluminum Brightener

The brightener is a diluted Hydro Fluoric Acid solution and other ingredients.

Alkaline

This is the opposite of acid on the pH Scale. A detergent with a pH of over thirteen can burn you as can an acid with a pH of three. Seven is neutral.

Aqueous degreaser tank

A tank filled with DI or RO Water and a water-based degreaser to clean and degrease aerospace parts.

B

Benefits

The advantage a prospect will receive when he or she gives you the order.

Bid

A bid is binding offer to supply goods according to specification at a fixed price.

Black Hole Situation

Your time goes in and never comes out. You're wasting your time.

Bloopers

Mistakes are a hard and costly learning experience.

Burning Desire

When a salesman wants to be No.1 so badly he or she will let nothing get in the way.

Buyer

A "buyer" is a person who processes orders but does not initiate them.

Buying Signal

When a prospect is agreeing with what the salesman is saying the salesman should stop talking and ask for the order.

C

Chemical punch

A boost to a chemical cleaner's power.

Cherry Picker

A "cherry picker" is a bucket on a mobile mechanical lift that raises one or two workers high enough to clean the tail and top of a jet airliner.

Closing

Closing is asking a prospect or customer to place an order.

Cold calls

When a salesman sees a potential customer and without knowing anything about them, stops in unannounced to make a presentation, cold.

Competitiveness

In sports or in selling, winning means everything. It's an attitude.

Competitive spirit

A salesman who wants to beat everyone to the top. This is the key to winning.

Competitors

Competitors are rival salesmen in your corporation and in your territory.

Confidentiality

Respecting each corporation's wishes not to have vendors tell their competitors what they are doing that would give their competitors an advantage.

Co-op ad

The cost of an ad in a local newspaper is split 50/50 between the vendor and the customer.

Corporate boxes

Corporate boxes are rooms in stadiums overlooking the field, court or rink, leased by corporations to entertain prospects and customers.

Cover all bases

Contacting everyone within the salesman's territory, letting them know what he sells and how he can be reached.

D

'Dark Energy'

It is an unseen force that counteracts gravity and causes the universe to expand faster.

Decision maker

A "decision maker" is person who has the authority to buy and who can initiate an order when a salesman asks.

De-Ionized Water ("DI Water")

Pure water after all the minerals and salts are filtered out.

Demonstration

Proof that what the salesman has told the prospect; is true. It is showmanship.

Determination

Keep going toward your goal and never give up.

Discounting

Reducing a company's selling price to get or keep business.

Distributors

Companies, usually local, that stock and sell products from many companies in the same general industry. Salesmen have small territories within a city.

Draw against commission

A salesman's monthly base pay to be deducted from commissions earned each month. The overage amount goes to the salesman.

E

Expense reports

Forms completed weekly or monthly to show business expenses incurred by a salesman in support of his or her sales activities.

Expert Witness Testimony

Testimony by a chemist that a floor finish meets or exceeds industry standards as it pertains to slip-coefficient in a "slip and fall" case.

F

Features

Features are the unique nuts and bolts of a product that produce benefits to the prospect or customer.

Federal Government

In most cases, federal government buys on a bid basis for the military and other departments.

Fill-ins

Fill-ins are orders that replace goods that have been sold, bringing the inventory back up to the "basic stock" level.

Flip chart

A "flip chart" is a sales prop used as a presentation guide.

'Fourth Dimension'
This refers to the "force" we can't see, but can make the *difference* in selling.

G

Gifts
A small token of appreciation, usually before the Christmas holidays, for the good business relationship a salesman has with his customers.
Goals
A goal is something without which you have no destination and will never get there.

I

International sales
Sales made to companies outside the United States of America.
In the Red
When a salesman's draw amount (set monthly pay) exceeds commissions earned.

M

Market place awareness
A salesman's knowledge of his competitors, their products and pricing in his or her territory and how they compare.
Master Salesman
A "street smart" salesman who has sold enough through the test of time to have earned the honor of being called: "Master Salesman."
Material Safety Data Sheets
List of ingredients required by the Environmental Protection Agency to accompany all chemical shipments.
Minefield of selling
These are distractions that impede a salesman's effectiveness.
Motivation
Motivation is a personal force that inspires action toward a goal.
"Murphy's Law"
"Anything that can go wrong will."

N

Name dropping
Telling a prospect that a major well known customer is using his product to add prestige to the product and imply that because of this, he should buy it too.

National customers
National customers are those that have branch plants in several states.

New line
New products introduced on a seasonal basis.

O

Organization
Systemize the tools of selling. Prioritize your actions.

Outside salesman
An "outside salesman's" territory is away from the home office and whose effectiveness depends largely upon his own decisions and salesmanship.

P

Perception
The appearance of a thing that is contrary to the fact.

Planning
Thinking ahead and organizing actions that are the most efficient in achieving a goal.

Prime selling time
Prime selling time is when your prospects are open for business.

Pricing knowledge
Knowing the standard pricing, quantity price breaks, discounts of all products you sell in addition to knowing the competitive prices.

pH
The symbol used to describe the acidity or alkalinity of a chemical solution on a scale of 0 (more acid) to 14 (more alkaline). Seven is neutral.

Prioritize
Prioritize sales calls in order of importance.

Product knowledge
Product knowledge is learning everything about your product's "features and benefits" and how to demonstrate the products effectively.

Prospect calls

Sales calls on companies a salesman wants to sell. (Sales to new customers are 100 percent increase)

"Pyramid of Selling"

The "Pyramid" illustrates the progression of factors necessary to complete a sale.

R

RO Water

Reverse Osmosis drinking water or pure water is produced from salt water by reversing and stopping the osmotic process by applying pressure, forcing the salt water through a membrane; an extremely fine filter. The membrane allows passage of water molecules, but not salt molecules.

Re-stocking charge

A penalty charged to the customer for returning goods for other than defect reasons.

S

Salesman

A salesman is a man or woman who sells goods and services to earn a living.

Sales Manager

A sales manager is man or woman from field sales who has earned the job of hiring, coaching and assisting his or her salesmen in selling the big prospects, and to help when needed. The overall job is to greatly increase sales in his or her region.

Sales tools

A vehicle, samples, order pad, pen and expertise in salesmanship.

"The salmon are running"

This is the busiest buying time of the year for your industry.

Samples

Tools of the trade must be kept in perfect condition.

"Scrub-Off"

"Scrub-Off" is a competitive contest using two Tenant 550 Riding Scrubbers to determine the better of two competing flight deck cleaners.

"Sell the sizzle"

Sell the emotional benefits, not the nuts and bolts.

Shipping charges

Cost of shipping the product to a customer.

Slacking the line

When fishing, if you "slack the line", you will lose the fish. The same is true in selling.

Slip and fall litigations

A lawsuit filed by a lawyer on behalf of a person who slipped and fell in a store or other public facility.

"Spiff"

A "spiff" is a prize or incentive, usually monetary, used to motivate salesmen to sell one company's products over competitive products.

Straight commission

Forgoing a "draw" and receiving only commissions earned.

"Street Smart"

Being "street smart," is knowledge of everything that is going on in your territory and how to use this knowledge effectively in selling yourself to the top.

T

Terms

Payment due date for merchandise received. Net 30, means full payment is due within thirty days. Two percent, 10, net 30, is a 2 percent discount if paid within ten days otherwise bill is due in full in thirty days.

'The Force'

In a sales context, "The force" is the elusive "fourth dimension" that we can't see or teach because it is elusive and personal, but which might be called "salesmanship."

Trial close

The salesman asks for the order when he senses a "buying signal" before the end of his presentation.

V

Value added

Other benefits a buyer will receive in addition to the product.

W

War stories

A salesman's story of how a great sale was accomplished.

Work ethic

Doing the best you can consistently every day.

About the Author

Robert H. Felgen was born in Oak Park, Illinois and worked in the sales profession in the Chicago area and the Midwest as a young man. Bob graduated from Lake Forest College with a Bachelor of Arts Degree in Economics. Bob "lettered" in baseball in high school and four years in college.

Bob Felgen is a "street smart" Master Salesman, Sales Manager and Vice President of National Accounts. Bob sold a wide variety of products to prospects and customers in almost every state in the United States and has sold industrial chemicals in California for thirty years. Bob spent five years as Aircraft Sales Manager, selling aircraft cleaning chemicals to the military and the major airlines.

Bob Felgen has been selling for over four decades and has learned the *secrets that make the difference* between a good salesman and being *"The Best Salesman."*

In this book, Bob shares his *"selling secrets"* with other professional salesmen and sales managers who have the *desire* and the *"work ethic"* to be *"The Best Salesman" and "The Best Sales Manager."*

Bob Felgen at United Airlines Maintenance Operations Center in San Francisco, CA

Bob believes selling is extremely interesting and exciting as you are an expert in your field. When you are recognized as an expert by your major customers, word gets around the industry. Bob was called and asked if he would give a "solvent replacement" presentation to a room full of scientists at the Jet Propulsion Laboratory on the solvent situation in the industry, due to new legislation. Bob agreed, as it was a great honor. They were especially interested in one of his company's water-based solvent replacement chemicals that had been tested, approved and was being used at most of the major aerospace companies in place of the solvent that had been banned.

Jet Propulsion Laboratory
California Institute of Technology
Pasadena, California

JPL Control Room

Courtesy NASA/JPL-Caltech

Bob and his wife, Ann, have a home in Laguna Niguel, California.

Index

978-0-595-40872-6
0-595-40872-9

www.ingramcontent.com/pod-product-compliance
Lightning Source LLC
Chambersburg PA
CBHW030949180526
45163CB00002B/718